Law on the Midway

Frank L. Ellsworth

Law on the Midway

The Founding of the
University of Chicago Law School

The Law School of the University of Chicago
Chicago, Illinois

Distributed by
The University of Chicago Press, Chicago 60637
The University of Chicago Press, Ltd., London

Printed in the United States of America
82 81 80 79 78 77 987654321

FRANK L. ELLSWORTH is assistant dean of
the Law School and lecturer in the
Social Sciences Collegiate Division of the
University of Chicago.

Library of Congress Cataloging in Publication Data

Ellsworth, Frank L
   Law on the Midway.

   Bibliography: p.
   Includes index.
   1.   Chicago. University. Law School—History.
I.   Title.
KF292.C4514E5   340'.07'1177311   77–78777
ISBN 0–226–20608–4

Contents

Acknowledgments

Numerous colleagues on the Midway have provided assistance over the period of this study which I wish to acknowledge. I am grateful to Robert L. McCaul who gave generously of his time and wisdom from the earliest discussion of the study and whose constant encouragement and support were essential to its completion. Innumerable persons have provided facts and ideas which have influenced the writing of this book, including Stanley N. Katz, Max Rheinstein, Walter J. Blum, Cyril O. Houle, Soia Mentschikoff, Sheldon Tefft, and Philip B. Kurland. Edward H. Levi posed questions in his response to my earliest outline which proved central to the work. Phil C. Neal and Norval Morris have generously allowed the time necessary to conduct the study and have been constant supporters of all aspects of my work.

Albert M. Tannler, archives research specialist in the Department of Special Collections, The Joseph Regenstein Library at the University of Chicago, provided immeasurable assistance. His interest in the archives of the university and the mysteries contained therein is contagious, and I am indebted to him. Clark A. Elliott, assistant curator of the Harvard University Archives in the Widener Memorial Library, was helpful in directing me to materials in the Harvard archives.

I am grateful to Artie Scott and Helen S. Howe for their help in the preparation of the manuscript.

Finally I wish to give special acknowledgment to two men: Lawrence A. Cremin, Frederick A. P. Barnard Professor and president of Teachers College, Columbia University, who introduced me to the history of American education; and my father, Clayton S. Ellsworth, Michael O. Fisher Professor Emeritus of History at the College of Wooster, who has re-

sponded critically to the manuscript in its various stages and to whom this book is dedicated.

Introduction

The University of Chicago Law School was founded in response to rapid and significant changes within American society in the 1890s. As that society became increasingly complex, the legislative and regulatory role of government extended into new areas of social and economic concern. Reform movements proliferated, together with confidence in the role of law as a lever to social justice.

The shortcomings of a society, as evident in economic, political, educational, and social institutions, were loudly voiced by reformers, frequently with a sense of moral outrage. Traditional institutions and processes were questioned and challenged. Adaption to new stituations was slowly attained and usually incomplete. Problems appeared in all aspects of society: federal and city government, big corporations, public transportation, communications, urban and agrarian living, banking, administration of justice, immigration, to name but a few. Extensive legislation was enacted to ameliorate problems, and thus a new body of law emerged.

Law and lawyers were not immune to the criticisms of reformers. Distrust of lawyers had been fashionable in varying degrees in earlier American history. The elitism of the late eighteenth- and early nineteenth-century bar described by Tocqueville and others collided with the notion inherent in Jacksonian democracy that efforts to limit entry into the bar or to establish standards within the professions were undemocratic. Following the Civil War, the legal profession was in a serious state of disarray, and criticism of the lawyer heightened in intensity. Traditional apprenticeship requirements were abolished and attempts at formal legal education diminished. Organized bar associations floundered as requirements for ad-

1

mission to the bar disappeared. The numerous scandals in all layers of American society in the 1890s did little to enhance the image of the lawyer or the law. Lawyers and judges were considered the pawns of capitalists and politicians. Massive developments in the body of law following the Civil War compounded the situation. With increased attention to human rights came the emancipation of married women, recognition of labor unions, prison reforms, and attempts to modify select portions of the law. Urban living brought the need for different ways of regulating society and administering justice. Corporation and railroad law was born out of the phenomena of business trusts and new modes of transportation. With the attempts at reform through legislation came codes.

Perhaps the most important factor affecting the law and the lawyer was the latter's major client, modern business. Lawyers had to understand developments in insurance, manufacturing, railroads, the telegraph, the telephone, as well as the laws affecting these developments. Skills and knowledge previously unheard of were required. To many observers law had ceased being a learned profession and had itself become big business. The independent lawyer, trained in the past by means of apprenticeship, was a fading phenomenon. Large city law firms emerged and the era of specialization began. During no previous period in the country's history had the nature of the law and the role of the lawyer changed so dramatically.

In the midst of these changes many reformers perceived the law as a panacea for the ills of society. The need for change was urged in law enforcement, criminal law, legislation, administration of law, preventive justice, and professionalization of lawyers. Respect for the law, the reformers claimed, would diminish social laxity and commercial and public frauds. The functions of the lawyer were to be commensurate with the polity, civilization, and indeed the destiny of the country. Toward the end of the century the American Bar Association, attempting to improve the negative image of the profession, spoke increasingly of law in terms of restoration and reconstruction. If the law was to provide a major remedy for the ills in society, the law schools had to assume new responsibilities. For if the future man of law was to be equipped to restore

and to reconstruct, the law schools would have to provide adequate training. The problem was how to define the purpose and nature of legal education.

Despite the rapid expansion in the number of law students and law schools in the 1890s, few schools reflected the need for departing from conventional practices. Proprietary law schools thrived. Few schools offered adequate training for even the traditional practice of law. With the growth of the cities came the growth of urban law schools. With the rise of land-grant and state institutions of higher education, with the increase in proprietary law schools and the development of evening and correspondence schools, legal education, too often of inferior quality, became available to everyone. The common denominator of legal education had become mediocrity.

Standards for admission, graduation, and admission to the bar were low. For most members of the bar, the growing number of law students was an economic threat as well as a leveling force to the proud traditions of the past. Law students were viewed as bold and unscrupulous, overcrowding the bar and bringing scandal and disgrace to the profession. Law school curricula were hardly designed to challenge students intellectually or to prepare them for the demands of a changing profession and society. The conventional content of legal education was geared to the technicalities essential for starting practice. Instruction in jurisprudence, comparative and international law, and legal reasoning was rarely found. Courses in public law were confined to criminal and constitutional law. Administrative law was ignored. Other academic disciplines such as political science, history, sociology, and economics were felt to be inappropriate for law school curricula. Instruction was at the undergraduate level, and for most schools a high school diploma was not required.

The deficiencies of legal education were listed by the American Bar Association in an 1890 report by its Committee on Legal Education. In comparison with standards for other professions, the standards for the legal profession were inferior, the report asserted. Although laws existed in most states concerning the practice of medicine, dentistry, and pharmacy, none existed for the practice of law. Requirements for admission to most schools were minimal; in many cases the law

school had become a loafer's paradise. Toward the turn of
the century the newly formed American Association of Law
Schools and the State Board of Law Examiners began to talk
about lifting the standards of the profession but met with
resistance from the organized bar and the schools.
In 1890 most lawyers received their training through self-
education and apprenticeship. By 1900 this situation was no
longer the case. The profession moved cautiously away from
traditional methods and slowly acknowledged that a more
comprehensive training might be desirable because of the
increased complexity of law. The early attempts at university
law schools had been notably unsuccessful, and proprietary
schools, which were merely offshoots of law offices, arose to
fill the void the academic institutions failed to satisfy. As the
law schools within colleges and universities became stronger,
several models, notably at Harvard and Columbia, were held
up for emulation.

Certain issues emerged during this time which served as
topics of discussion in educational and professional circles.
One concerned the duration of law study. Existing traditions
and economic demands argued for short periods of study; the
young lawyer could learn how to be a lawyer after beginning
practice. At the same time, demands for higher standards, a
recognition of the increased complexity of the law, and concern for academic respectability of legal education within
university communities argued for at least two or three years
of study. Yet the competition from proprietary schools was
formidable: commercial standards were more appealing than
scholastic standards. Few universities were successful in de-
fining and implementing professional legal education. Most
were content with either a smattering of courses at the undergraduate level or with a narrowly defined series of practical
and technical law courses.

The innovations by Christopher Columbus Langdell at Harvard became a watershed for American legal education. In
1872 the period of study at Harvard was extended to two
years; in 1876, with the crucial support of President Charles W.
Eliot, a third year was added. Although several schools eventually followed Harvard's example by providing more than a
one-year curriculum, most law schools remained undisturbed.

Harvard, under the leadership of Langdell and Eliot, also took the lead in improving standards of admission to law schools. But most schools designed their programs to attract students and then admitted anyone accordingly. The issue at Harvard and elsewhere had financial implications: higher standards might result in fewer students, thus lower revenue. Nevertheless, Langdell started his drive in 1875, and ten years later prospective students needed either a B.A. degree or had to be qualified to enter Harvard's senior class for admission to Harvard Law School. At Columbia the effort met with opposition until 1899, when the faculty voted to admit, beginning in 1903, only college graduates or others with equivalent backgrounds. Yale and most other eastern colleges were slow to accept the notion of law as graduate study largely because of opinions which were based on the traditional notion of the supremacy of the collegiate experience.

The curriculum established by Joseph Story at Harvard and elaborated by Langdell became in time the standard model for law schools, although most schools offered considerably less. Yet the study of law was essentially technical and practical even at Harvard. In the 1890s questions were raised concerning the desirability of a closer relation between the liberal arts and the emerging social sciences and law. But courses in legal history, administrative law, jurisprudence, and comparative law were felt to dilute the curriculum. Instruction in the theory of legislation and criminology were proper for political scientists but not for lawyers.

Although scientific scholarship as expounded by Langdell maintained that law was a science—that the contents of the law could be made consistent through analytical scrutiny—most lawyers and professors viewed "legal science" as a misnomer. The significance of the case system of study fathered by Langdell was hotly contested, and the Yale system, the Dwight method, and other traditional methods of teaching were all evident in the 1890s. Perhaps the most significant contribution of the Harvard model as defined by Langdell and Eliot was that legal education became firmly established in university life.

Reform in American society was a major theme of the World's Congress Auxiliary held in 1893 in conjunction with

the Columbian Exposition on the Midway in Chicago. Over 5,900 speakers spoke at 1,283 sessions on topics including suffrage, law reform and jurisprudence, civil service reform, and city government. The attention of people around the world focused on Chicago's "White City," which itself was a work of art. A nearby enterprise, the recently established University of Chicago, also attracted considerable attention, due largely to the efforts of its first president, William Rainey Harper. His was a different institution, a great urban university springing overnight from the marshlands off the Midway Plaisance as a neighbor to the colossal world's fair.

The design of Harper's university was grandiose and excitingly different in American higher education. His original plan for the university in 1891 called for a law school. In view of Harper's dream of a new university, it is not surprising that he wanted to include legal education, nor that he chose to consider something different. Harper's Law School, which opened October 1, 1902, would be at once both eclectic and innovative—characteristics not uncommon on the Midway— and certainly would attempt to reflect in its mission the demands and problems of a rapidly changing society which placed heavy strains on the system of law and thereby on the preparation of lawyers.

1   The Rise of Harper's University

Rumblings of Reform
The Chicago Legal Community
toward the End of the Century

The prospects for reform in American society through the law were frequently expressed toward the end of the nineteenth century by politicians, reform leaders, muckrakers, and occasionally by lawyers and academics. Following several decades in which American society had been lulled into accepting corruption and decadence as norms of American life, cries for change were increasingly heard as the 1890s passed. The moral and social degeneration of society seemed at hand. The law was viewed by many as a panacea for reform. In an 1894 address before the youthful American Bar Association, Woodrow Wilson, professor of jurisprudence and political economy at Princeton, maintained that law had an urgent role in the regeneration of society. Yet everywhere the lawyer was viewed with great suspicion. What was needed, Wilson insisted, were prophets and change, not barristers and judgment.[1]

A reflection of the growing concern for the possibility of reform through law was evident in a series of "Reform Congresses" held in connection with the Columbian Exposition in 1893. Throughout America newspapers turned their attention to the numerous activities held in the grand buildings constructed along the Midway Plaisance on the marshlands in south Chicago. The congresses, conceived by Judge Charles Carroll Bonney, a prominent member of the Chicago Bar, were intended "to promote future progress by the fraternal cooperation of the enlightened minds of all countries." Sessions were held on suffrage, law reform and jurisprudence, civil service reform, and city government.[2]

The Reform Congresses were arranged by leaders of the
Chicago Bar Association, which had just experienced a mild
revitalization and had heard occasional rumbles for reform.
Founded in 1873, the association had been heralded by Myra
Bradwell, editor of the *Chicago Legal News,* as an effective and
necessary means for enhancing the standards of the bar: "the
disreputable shysters who now disgrace the profession could
be driven from it."[3] A careful reading of the history of the
Chicago Bar Association as told by Herman Kogan, however,
calls in question the effectiveness of this organization before
the turn of the twentieth century.

Mrs. Bradwell, who fought sexual discrimination in a losing
battle for her own admission to the bar, was from the earliest
days of the *Chicago Legal News* vocal in exposing the corruption of the local bar. Hardly any major or minor issue escaped
her editorial eye. Founded in 1868, this colorful publication
contained sundry items ranging from records of cases to calls
for "improvements in everything directly or indirectly connected with the practice of law."[4]

Perennial themes for Mrs. Bradwell, and ones common to
the reform literature of the time throughout the country, were
denunciation of low standards for admission to the bar, the ex-
posure of corruption and unprofessional work among judges
and lawyers, and the condemnation of tolerance of unlicensed
practitioners. Initially pleased with the attempts following the
Civil War to stiffen admission requirements for the bar and
thus "to decrease the vast number of incompetent people who
are yearly admitted to the bar," she complained soon after:
"The crude and vulgar course of study pursued in law offices
has been the means of placing the names of many very poor
lawyers upon the roll of the profession who, if they had taken
a thorough and well-digested course of reading, might have
been numbered among its most useful members."[5]

The objectives of the Chicago Bar Association echoed those
of other bar organizations; its rhetoric and practice, however,
unlike those of other organizations, are striking by their omis-
sion of any reference to the promotion of legal education or to
the science of jurisprudence. The bylaws of the Chicago association did call for a standing committee on legal education,
but the only effort by this group was the occasional attempt to

raise the standards of admission to the bar. Other state bar associations were to go beyond the rhetoric of their constitutions
by examining rigorously practices and standards of legal education. But the early years of the Chicago association were
undistinguished, and the major activity was admittedly social.[6]

Toward the end of the 1880s the association showed signs
of renewed life, as was true with other organized bar groups
in the nation. In a call to arms in 1886 James L. High, later to
become president of the organization, echoed criticisms of the
changing profession being made throughout the country:
"The scientific and philosophical is giving way to the money
making and commercial. The bar of this country is becoming
a sort of trades union, lacking even the elements of cohesion
which belong to most trades unions. The vicious system of an
elective judiciary and the unseemly scramble among lawyers
for every vacant judicial position are among the surest signs
of the decadence of the professional spirit. The bar is coming
to occupy no higher rank than that of ordinary business avoca-
tions!"[7]

Also in 1886, as interest in raising the standards of the profession became more evident, at least rhetorically, the city of
Chicago and the legal community were struck by the drama
of the Haymarket Square riot. For the following seven years,
until the pardon of several of the convicted rioters, the association was officially silent on the affair. Publicly the organization lauded Judge Joseph B. Gary, whose participation both as
presiding judge and as commentator following the trial, was
later judged to be an embarrassment for the Chicago legal
profession. Extensive discussions of the merits of the case and
of its political overtones were carried on by Chicago lawyers,
but few lawyers rose in defense of the alleged conspirators.[8]

The nineties were restless years for the Chicago legal community, which gradually acknowledged the unprofessional
handling and disposition of the case that initially had been
defended by many prominent Chicago lawyers. As the issue
began to subside, passions arose within the profession after
the murder of Mayor Carter H. Harrison in 1893 by a lawyer
angered over the mayor's selection of another person for the
position of corporation counsel. The young professional organization struggled to throw off the frontier image of back-

woods lawyers and to define the role of the lawyer in a changing, urban society.

Thus in 1893, with an economic depression on the immediate horizon, the Columbian Exposition soon to close, and
the glamour of international attention fast waning, the organized bar began to sink back into its traditional state of
apathy. One must note that the reform congresses of the exposition were not in the mainstream of concern for the
Chicago legal community. Indeed few of the notions expressed
at the congresses were radical. "The overall approach was
modern, however, and plainly geared to serve the needs of
current society. In the first place these men concentrated on
the welfare of the entire people, and tied political stability to
a reasonable degree of economic equality in an industrial age.
Second, lawyers and reformers sanctioned a positive role for
local government in maintaining social and economic democracy."[9]

Although the forum provided by the reform congresses was
limited, many of the questions posed were common to discussions throughout the growing urban areas in the country:
problems of wealth, civil service reform, city government, and
forms of municipal finances; simplification of pleading, aban-
donment of the distinction between common law and equity,
and the issue of codification versus adherence to the traditions
of common law.

Perhaps the most notable accomplishment of the Chicago
Bar Association prior to the turn of the century was its mild
campaign to raise the standards of admission to the bar.[10] The
reaction to these efforts was mixed. Thomas A. Moran, president of the Chicago College of Law, cited the precedent that
men who could not spell well and who were without education
could become distinguished lawyers. "I had a young man in
my classes who was not a good grammarian, could not spell
all the words in the spelling book, worked at plumbing days
and studied law nights, but had an excellent legal mind and
will make his mark in the profession."[11] No doubt many lawyers shared Moran's opinions.

Finally in 1897, under the leadership of Julius Rosenthal,
the association convinced the Illinois Supreme Court to establish a State Board of Law Examiners. In his brief Rosenthal

observed: "Not even a fundamental knowledge of the three R's is necessary for admission. . . . The lazy student desirous of becoming a professional man seeks the law as the easiest entrance gate."[12] Although the State Board of Law Examiners was to have limited effect on raising standards of admission, its establishment did indicate what the bar could do if it chose to exert its influence. One thing the bar had not done up until this time was to show any great interest in legal education.

Legal Education at
The Old University of Chicago

Although Chicago, like New York and Philadelphia, now numbered over one million people, no nationally known or even adequate law school existed in Chicago in the 1890s. Several attempts to provide legal education had been made, and several proprietary schools had been launched. In 1847 some Chicago lawyers and judges invited a downstate lawyer, John J. Brown, to Chicago to give informal instruction in law. In addition to lectures by Brown on the fundamentals of law, other lectures were given occasionally by practicing lawyers. "A teacher with piercing eyes," according to Kogan, "a massive shock of hair, and vehement gestures," Brown was described as a " 'retiring and misanthropic man, undoubtedly the greatest master of withering and remorseless irony, when aroused, of satirical and scornful gibe then at the Chicago Bar, and of sarcasm that, when given full rein, had something almost sardonic in it.' "[13] An informal study group of Chicago lawyers was formed in 1848 and gave rise to the Chicago Law Institute in 1857, which was furthered by a gift of several hundred law books from Julius Rosenthal.

The first attempt to provide formal legal education in Chicago occurred in 1856 with the founding of the old University of Chicago by Stephen A. Douglas with funds provided largely by prominent members of the Baptist church. The earliest mission of the university was to educate young men for the Baptist ministry. Students were drawn primarily from the Midwest. Three years after the University was established at 3400 Cottage Grove, a law department was founded by Thomas Hoyne, a well-known lawyer who served as justice

of the Probate Court of Cook County, United States district
attorney, and United States marshal.[14]

The first catalogue of the old University of Chicago Law
Department, that of 1859–60, lists Douglas as president of the
university and indicates that twenty-two of the thirty-six trustees of the institution were lawyers—the rest were predomi-
nately ministers. The trustees represented the foremost citizens
of Chicago. Requirements for admission to both the law department and the rest of the university were nonexistent. The
predominance of legal education in the life of the old university
became evident in the first year of the law department: of the
178 students enrolled in the university for that year, 48 were
law students. The majority came from Illinois, Iowa, Wisconsin, Kentucky, Michigan, Pennsylvania, and Kansas, a fact
reflecting the paucity of law schools in the frontier territory.
Pressured by the vocal feminist, Myra Bradwell, the university
agreed to admit women into the law department, contrary to
the conventions of the time in American law schools. Located
at 80 South Dearborn in downtown Chicago, in order to be
close to the courts, the law department drew its faculty from
the local bench and bar.

The curriculum was conventional. At no time in the history
of the department was the program more than an elementary
college-level "bread and butter" curriculum. Books utilized,
according to the catalogues, were Blackstone's *Commentaries*,
Bouvier's *Institutes*, Kent's *Commentaries*, Stephen's *Commentaries*, and Wooddeson's *Lectures*. The course of study
was skimpy, assuming completion of the curriculum as outlined annually: law of real property; equity; personal property, personal rights and contracts; commercial and maritime
law; evidence, pleadings, and practice; criminal law; and constitutional law and the law of nations. Although the curriculum expanded occasionally with courses such as domestic
relations and real estate, the actual program of study was
never intended to teach more than the bare essentials necessary for survival in the initial years of law practice. The
department represented the traditional adjunct to the law
office, the proprietary law school.

The objective of the university's trustees regarding legal
education was set forth directly in the catalogue: to make the

course of study as practical as possible. The trustees also
expressed their civic aspirations for the school. The university
was to be an institution that would have a profound effect on
the city and become an important ingredient in the social
fabric. "The University of Chicago had its origins in the con-
victions of its founders, of the necessity of such an Institution," the annual catalogues maintained, "both to the city of
Chicago and the great country to which it is so ultimately
linked."

Despite the noble hopes of the founders, many of whom
were leading jurists and members of the bar, the history of this
proprietary law school is uneven and undistinguished. Thomas
M. Hoyne, Jr., son of the founder and himself a graduate of the
class of 1866, described his experience, revealing the physical
limitations of the institution as well as the lack of rigor of the
study:

> The Law School was located on the fourth floor of the
> Larmon Block. It occupied one room. The floor was bare
> and the furniture consisted of a plain table on a slightly
> elevated platform and a collection of wooden chairs.
> Fortunately, there were enough of these to allow each
> student two if desired. The faculty consisted of Professors
> Henry Booth and Harvey B. Hurd. Possibly we may have
> had an occasional lecture by some prominent member of the
> bar. Professor Booth was the life and spirit of the institution.
> . . . Students were at liberty to attend all classes without
> regard to the order of studies and if they were able to pass
> the final examination, graduated. The main thing was to get
> through with the work as quickly as possible.[15]

Problems plagued the institution from the beginning and
prompted the trustees to look beyond the university for means
of stabilization. On October 8, 1871, a fire destroyed the Law
School building and, according to the old university's historian, Koenitzer, "scattered the students among the other
Western Law Schools."[16] By 1872 studies were resumed, and
negotiations were initiated by Hoyne with Northwestern University in the hope that an affiliation might resolve continued
financial problems.

Discussion about the establishment of a law department at

Northwestern had begun in 1854, three years after Northwestern was founded by the Methodists, and continued until
1859, when the Northwestern trustees approved a committee's
recommendation to open a law department. The opening, however, was delayed by the announcement of the new law department at the old University of Chicago.[17] Discussions concerning a joint effort continued between the two institutions,
and on June 24, 1873, the law department of the University of
Chicago was "declared to be also the Law Department of the
Northwestern University." Each institution was to appoint
three members from its trustees who, along with the two presidents, would constitute an executive committee. Financially,
each institution was to provide not less than $2,000 per year.
If either institution were to default, the control of the law
department was automatically to pass to the institution that
kept the contract. Reaction to the offspring of the two institutions was mixed. The *Chicago Legal News* predicted "that two
institutions like this cannot run a law school in partnership for
any length of time" but voiced the optimistic belief, shared by
many, "that the course of lectures in this College will be fully
equal if not superior to any in the United States."[18]

The next year the law department became known as "The
Union College of Law of the Chicago University and the
Northwestern University," and a two-year course was announced. The faculty doubled and the school was remodeled
"upon a basis which will give it undivided sympathy at the
bar."[19] Despite the fact that the law department at the old
University of Chicago had become the strongest part of the
university, as evident in its top billing in 1868 over the college,
things never went smoothly between the college and the law
department due to management and financial weaknesses.[20]
Only three years after the joint venture began, the two universities contributed $1,000 each, and in 1877 the Union
College of Law was run solely on the revenues from tuition.
Students were easily attracted, largely because there were no
entrance requirements and a degree from the Union College
provided automatic admission to the Illinois bar. But the rigor
and substance of the education were questionable, even after
the coalition with Northwestern. A member of the class of

1883, Frank H. Childs, candidly noted that "the aim of many students seemed to be merely to put in the required time without showing such dense ignorance as to jeopardize their standing in the College. Pranks were of almost daily occurrence."[21]

Yet it is important to note that, despite the inadequacies of the Union College of Law, the school filled an educational void in one of the nation's largest cities. Consistent with the traditions of most American law schools of the time, Union College never claimed to be other than a proprietary institution or intended to provide more than the practical rudiments of law to young people who were admitted without previous training. What was necessary, argued the trustees, was a legal education which extended the traditional notion of apprenticeship and which would train lawyers to fill the constantly increasing number of positions available each day in the growing industrial city of Chicago.

Nearly one thousand people graduated from Union. Of these almost four hundred practiced in Chicago. Childs recalled that of his senior class of seventy-five students "quite a large percentage later attained mention in *Who's Who in America*. The best known of them was William Jennings Bryan."[22] Writing in 1889 on the history of Union College of Law, James E. Babb, a member of the class of 1884, suggested that Union alumni not only in Chicago but in central, southern, western, and northwestern states have "laid its foundations deep in the social fabric. The Law School already feels the strong pulse of this great power." Babb mentioned four alumni who were presently on the bench, including the chief justice of the Appellate Court, two masters in chancery, and the city attorney. "Others stand in the front rank of the Chicago Bar and others still are among Chicago's representative business men."[23]

As in all law schools of the period, the life of Union College of Law centered around several important faculty, all of whom were drawn from active practice or from the bench and taught part-time.[24] Serving as dean from 1859 to 1891, Henry Booth came to Chicago from Poughkeepsie, where he had been a professor at the State and National Law School. Under the

new Illinois Constitution of 1870, Booth was elected a judge
of the Circuit Court of Cook County and served in that capac-
ity through 1882.

The other major faculty member was the founder, Thomas
Hoyne, who, like Booth, was active in Chicago civic and political activities. Unlike Booth, who received his legal education
at Yale, Hoyne was the product of the traditional apprenticeship system, having studied in the New York City office of
John Brinkerhoff. Hoyne was almost elected mayor of Chicago
in 1876 on a "Citizens Ticket" but lost to the Democratic
candidate following a recount. Hoyne did serve as a county
judge and a U.S. district attorney and was an active member of
the young Chicago Bar Association.

Joining Booth the first year were Grant Goodrich and John
M. Wilson, two Cook County judges. Other well-known
names included Harvey B. Hurd, who compiled and rewrote
the Illinois statutes from 1869 to 1874, and who was the major
draftsman of the Torrens Land Title Registration Act of 1898
and the Juvenile Court Act of 1899; Nathan S. Davis, who was
founder of the American Medical Association and one of the
founders and dean of the Northwestern Medical School; and
Lyman Trumbull, who served on the Illinois Supreme Court
and also as a United States congressman and senator from
Illinois.

The problems which beleaguered Union College of Law
throughout its history culminated in 1886. Beset by misman-
agement and lack of harmony among the University of
Chicago trustees, the institution closed on June 16, following
foreclosure by Union Mutual Life Insurance Company in Port-
land, Maine. The accumulated debts of the old University of
Chicago totaled $150,000 and were funded in a five-year trust
held by the Union Mutual Life Insurance Company with an
8 percent interest. Unable to pay off the indebtedness, which
increased each year, the trustees went into extensive litigation.[25] Through legal maneuverings the trustees claimed the
initial contract for the trust invalid, maintaining that the university had exceeded its powers in entering the agreement.
The reaction of the public to these maneuverings was negative,
and the institution came under heavy fire. In 1886, in a last-
minute effort to save the dying university, the trustees elected

William Rainey Harper to the presidency. Harper declined the offer. The *Chicago Daily News* declared: "It now looks as though the university had lost not only its property but its character."[26] The Baptist church was equally dismayed and embarrassed. An editorial in its Chicago-published newspaper, *Standard*, prophesied: "We say for the Baptists of America, that they will never again try to build up a great institution of learning upon borrowed money."[27]

Under the initial agreement between the two institutions, Northwestern now assumed complete control over the law department. On July 1, 1891, a new contract with the Union College of Law provided that all property be transferred to Northwestern "in perpetual trust for the sole use of the Union College of Law, hereafter known as Northwestern University Law School." Unlike the remaining alumni of the old University of Chicago, who eventually became alumni of William Rainey Harper's new University of Chicago, all law graduates, as specified in the contract of June 24, 1873, became alumni of Northwestern University Law School.

Ironically, the interest demonstrated by the Chicago legal community in legal education began to stir as the affairs of the Union College of Law became increasingly tangled and its future doubtful. The board of regents of Union, as listed in the last catalogue, that of 1883–84, included district court judges, Illinois Supreme Court justices, and leaders of the Chicago bar. The chairman of the executive committee of Union's board of trustees (he was also president of the old University of Chicago) was Galusha Anderson, a distinguished Chicago lawyer who was vitally interested in legal education. Anderson was also professor of international law in the prelaw program at Union. As President, Anderson "inherited a divided constituency and an alienated public."[28] Other trustees who played central roles at Union College of Law included Eli B. Felsenthal, R. R. Donnelley, and C. C. Kohlstaat. As is often the case, little is known about the dissension among the trustees that continued throughout the history of Union. It is interesting to speculate, however, whether curricular issues were involved as well as the obvious financial ones. As will be seen later, Anderson, Felsenthal, and Kohlstaat were important counselors to William Rainey Harper as he worked out the de-

tails of his vision of a new law school on the Midway that was to differ sharply with the practically oriented, college-level program at Union and then at Northwestern.

Despite the support of distinguished members of the profession who recognized the need for legal education, Union College of Law was short-lived, a common characteristic of the proprietary and independent law schools that sprang up following the Civil War. Many disappeared completely. Others were absorbed by institutions, giving rise to university law schools such as Yale's. In many instances all that was done was to attach the university name to an existing institution which continued substantially unchanged as an out-department of the university. Sheldon Tefft, James Parker Hall Professor Emeritus at the University of Chicago, suggests that the goals of most of these mergers were "to outline the institutions' claims to be a university rather than a college; to enhance the revenues of the institutions and also of course to provide a solid preparation for careers in the law."[29]

The nineties were "critical years" for the newly founded Northwestern Law School according to James A. Rahl and Kurt Schwerin.[30] The failure to integrate the law school into university life resulted in instability in the academic program and the administration of the former Union College of Law. With the retirement in 1891 of Dean Booth, who had been the sustaining force at Union, Northwestern experienced three part-time deans in close succession as the institution tried to determine the purpose of a university law school. Serving for only one year, federal judge Henry W. Blodgett, the target earlier of much abuse by the Chicago Bar Association, left in 1892 to arbitrate the seal-fur dispute between the United States and England. The trustees then designated Henry Wade Rogers as acting dean. Rogers was serving at the time as Northwestern's president and had come from the University of Michigan Law School where he had served as dean. Active and vocal in the reform movements in legal education within the American Bar Association, Rogers apparently found some time from his double university responsibilities to make at least one major contribution to the law school during his six-year term. In a reorganization effort in 1892 he increased the number of full-time resident professors from one to four.

Among the new men he attracted to the faculty were Nathan
Abbott, Edward A. Harriman, Blewett Lee, and Julian W.
Mack. Two of these four, Lee and Mack, were later enticed
away to help found Harper's law school. Abbott went to
Stanford to carry out a similar function. Rogers left Northwestern to become dean at Yale Law School in 1900, where he
helped to change a collegiate, proprietary law department into
a professional one. In 1898 Judge Peter S. Grosscup, judge of
the United States Circuit Court and later the Circuit Court of
Appeals, was appointed dean.

The law school quarters at Northwestern left much to be
desired. An expansion in 1893 into the Masonic Temple was
limited to a lecture hall, library and reading room, and a
students' room. Motivated by the movement on the east coast
to expand the law program to three years, the faculty asked
the university to do the same in 1894, noting that the legisla-
tures in Ohio and Wisconsin required three years. The *Northwestern Law Review* was first published in 1893 but ceased
in 1896 and did not begin again until 1906. Struggling for
definition in the nineties, lacking long-term leadership and
direction, Northwestern Law School awaited the turn of the
century and the leadership of John H. Wigmore before establishing itself as a professional school.

Thus the attempts to launch legal education in Chicago
following the Civil War met with little success, despite the
growing needs of the community and the increased interest
of civic leaders in establishing a law school with high educational standards. Although a handful of Illinois lawyers participated actively in various reform movements, most seemed to
have been indifferent to the many issues posed elsewhere that
stirred the profession—in particular, issues concerning legal
education. The city of Chicago had to wait until the energetic
William Rainey Harper began creating his university on the
South Side before the hopes for a nationally recognized professional law school were to be realized.

Harper and His University

"The law-making bodies of democracy are gradually losing
strength and prestige," William Rainey Harper declared in

the 1899 Charter Day address entitled "The University and Democracy" at the University of California. "Another quarter of a century of deterioration, another quarter of a century without radical modification of the present plan, will put popular government in a position which will be embarrassing in the extreme. Thus far democracy seems to have found no way of making sure the strongest men should be placed in control of the country's business."[31] For Harper, the first president of the University of Chicago, which was founded in 1891, the task of building instantly a great national university on the Midway was the highest of callings. Scholar, minister, teacher, student of the Old Testament, entrepreneur, public relations wizard, and prime intellectual force behind the Chautauqua movement, Harper had little patience with notions of education reflecting anything less than greatness or with a concept of a university whose mission was separate from the society from which it emerged.

"Education is the basis of all democratic progress," maintained Harper, whose institution had to "be born full-fledged" and would immediately rival Harvard and Johns Hopkins as a model of the American university. Harper's concept of a university was clearly articulated: "What is a university today? I accept, with modification, a common definition; a self-governing association of men for the purpose of study; an institution privileged by the state for the guidance of the people; an agency recognized by the people for resolving the problems of civilization which present themselves in the development of civilization."[32] The democratic function of education was essential to Harper's definition of higher education: "it is clear that everything points in one direction, namely toward the growing democratization of higher education work."[33] Like Thomas Jefferson and Charles Eliot before him, Harper believed that the university was to be an integral part of the public school system. But unlike Jefferson and Eliot, Harper's conception of a university called for a diversified mission which can best be characterized as grandiose.

The combination of notions both democratic and elite resulted in "Harper's Bazaar," as some journalists and critics described the new institution which sprang up in awesome

neogothic buildings on the muddy south Chicago flats. Harper's university included an extensive set of affiliated academies, a university extension program with correspondence courses, manual training schools, and a university press established to produce and to disseminate a steady stream of scholarly books and journals. These functions, new in American higher education, helped meet the democratic responsibilities as perceived by Harper. Yet elitism was not a concept foreign to Harper, who maintained that it "is the highest function of the university to prepare leaders and teachers for every field of activity."[34] Thus in a speech given in 1899 before the regents of the University of New York on "Waste in Higher Education," Harper declared: "I should not be surprised if, when all the facts are collected, it should prove true that 10 or 20 per cent of those who go out from colleges had better never have entered; better, I mean, for the men's own sake as well as that of the institution."[35]

Having written a comparative study of the prepositions in Latin, Greek, Sanskrit, and Gothic for his Ph.D. dissertation at Yale, and having taught Hebrew and biblical studies at the Baptist seminary in Morgan Park, at Vassar, and at Yale, Harper was a respected scholar of the Old Testament and, in particular, of Hebraic law. With missionary zeal and the rhetorical persuasion of a minister, Harper set out to create his university. He sometimes expressed his concept of a university in biblical terms:

The University is a priest established to act as mediator in the religion of democracy, wherever mediation may be possible; established to lead the souls of men and nations into close communications with the common soul of all humanity; established to stand apart from other institutions, and at the same time to mingle closely with the constituent elements of the people; established to introduce whosoever will into all the mysteries of the past and present, whether solved or unsolved. . . . the true university, the university of the future, is one the motto of which will be: Service for mankind wherever mankind is, whether within scholastic walls or without those walls and in the world at large. Some,

perhaps, many, will deny that democracy has a religion; but no one will deny that democracy has a philosopher; and the university, I contend, is the philosopher of democracy.[36]

The pragmatic Harper knew what he wanted and how to get it, as the entire story of the founding of the University of Chicago reveals. There had been other experimenters and experiments in higher education. Harper was determined single-handedly to improve on and, indeed, to surpass such efforts: Charles W. Eliot at Harvard; Andrew D. White at Cornell; Daniel Coit Gilman at Johns Hopkins; G. Stanley Hall at Clark; and David Starr Jordan at Stanford. Despite John D. Rockefeller's inclination to limit the new institution to merely a Baptist college, Harper had a grander plan. He described it to Rockefeller in terms of business trusts—language certainly not unfamiliar to the university's founder. Rockefeller had pursued Harper persistently and vigorously to become president, and Harper, raised in the little town of New Concord, Ohio, knew how to deal shrewdly with the nation's wealthiest man. Thus he queried Rockefeller in November, 1888, "Why should not this university erected at Chicago include as an organic part of it besides the theological seminary also various colleges throughout the West? . . . and let it be a university made up of a score of colleges with a large degree of uniformity in their management; in other words, an educational trust."[37]

Harper was impatient from the start in the hope that the university would represent excellence in an unprecedented diversity of academic programs and other activities. As if there were no plausible alternatives, he plunged ahead with his seemingly limitless objectives prior to the opening of the university in 1891. A small denominational college it was not to be. Writing to Rockefeller in August 1890, Harper dramatically insisted: "The denomination and indeed the whole country are expecting the University of Chicago to be from the very beginning an institution of the highest rank and character. Already it is talked of in connection with Yale, Harvard, Princeton, Johns Hopkins, the University of Michigan and Cornell. . . . Naturally we ought to be willing to begin small and to grow, but in these days when things are done so rapidly and with

the example of Johns Hopkins before our eyes, it seems a great pity to wait for growth when we might be born full-fledged."[38]

Harper expressed sharply his disappointment in colleagues who did not share his view and were reluctant to move away from the established patterns in education. One of the clearest statements of his aspirations, as well as of his strategy, is found in a letter to Thomas Wakefield Goodspeed on November 28, 1888: "if the thing you are wanting at Chicago is only a College, I have been working upon a wrong task . . . and the result will be that a College is all that we shall get. My only desire is to see the thing go through in as large a form as possible, and I am sure that unless we come out boldly and confidently for what we want, viz. a University of the highest character, having also a College, we shall lose ground and make a mistake."[39] The desire to experiment was an overriding one for Harper, who viewed all tasks, major or minor, with this foremost in mind. "No one can fail to see that our institutions of learning are as much trammelled by traditions embodying ideas which have been dead for decades," Harper observed in his August 1893 "Quarterly Statement," "as the church is trammelled by dogmas of which the real meaning has been forgotten."[40]

The design of the university that Harper had been formulating for some time in his mind was detailed in the *Official Bulletin No. 1* in 1891.[41] The university would have three divisions: the university proper (for traditional academic work), the university extension, and university publication work. The outline of the university proper included preparatory academies; undergraduate colleges of liberal arts, science, literature, and practical arts; affiliated colleges; a nonprofessional graduate school; and schools of divinity, law, medicine, engineering, pedagogy, fine arts, and music. Harper recommended a summer quarter that would allow the work of the university to go on throughout the year. Harper concluded his announcement of the plan of the university by listing twenty-six advantages of his creation, with the final one being that it would provide "for the administration of the institution in accordance with a truly American and a truly University spirit."[42] And so the University of Chicago came into being, born almost overnight, almost "full-fledged." Unhampered by traditions, pioneering on an educational frontier, an institution arose under the creative hand of Harper.

It would be several years before descriptions of Harper's university would be common, as writers and observers marveled at the activities on the Midway. But soon many attempts were made. In an article in *Scribner's Magazine* in 1895 novelist Robert Herrick posed the question of prototype and suggested the challenge which Harper willingly undertook:

> One seeks curiously in the system of the University of Chicago for the predominating type or ideal; is it the American college with its group of professional schools, or the English Oxford with its care for the individual soul, or the German university? . . . It is a truism that the most distinctive move in American college life of the last decade has been in the sudden interest in post-graduate study. But hitherto no Western institution, whether college or so-called university, has had the means to provide liberally for advanced studies. This open field, therefore, it has been the ambition of the University of Chicago, situated in the centre of a vast inland constituency of small colleges, to develop.[43]

Harper Reaches for Professional Education

The initial plan of Harper's university called for a natural growth of the institution, including the creation of professional schools. There were many expressions of this hope in his early negotiations with Rockefeller. This objective was not immediately attained, largely because of financial reasons and not because of any disregard for the initial plan.[44] Harper viewed professional schools as an integral part of the university just as such schools were viewed on the Continent, where law and medicine had been the earliest established university studies. Joseph H. Beale was to observe after coming to Chicago from Harvard that "Chicago is almost, if not quite, alone in having adopted this practice from the beginning."[45] Harper urged a closer identification of the professional schools and the universities. He was severely critical and yet optimistic about the nature of professional education: "The majority of law and medicine schools in this country are stock companies, organized for pecuniary profit; but within a short period a change has come, and we already see the beginnings of reorganization in every quarter." Unquestionably Harper wanted to be in the forefront of this movement. "This union of professional education with the university which is rapidly taking place in all the great centres of the country," Harper continued in a 1902 article in the *North American Review*, "means two things: (1) the uplifting of this work, its broadening, and its acceptance of higher ideas; (2) the separation, to a greater or less degree, of the control of this work from the particular professions."[46]

Harper's dream of his university ultimately won out over the rival ideas of others within the university. Thomas W. Goodspeed, who had examined the resources and inclinations of the Baptist community in the years following the death of the old University of Chicago, feared another failure. In a statement of concession in 1897, after differing with Harper while serving as fund-raiser and counsel to Rockefeller, Goodspeed confessed: "If my views had prevailed, we should have had in Chicago an institution located on a single block of ground with three of four small buildings, and the character of the institution would have been simply that of a small but respectable college. . . . we have an institution which in five years has taken a position beside the great universities of the country which have existed from 150 to 250 years."[47]

Although Rockefeller was to be extraordinarily generous, the first decade in the life of the university was difficult. Constant deficits plagued the institution, and the problems resulting from these deficits must be noted in order to understand the rise of the professional schools.[48] Richard J. Storr observes that the "causes of frustration and disenchantment were not imaginary. In the first year and long thereafter, the aspirations and resources of the University were far out of balance."[49] Goodspeed defended the deficits in 1897:

. . . we have been laying the foundations for a very great enterprise. It was greater than we, ourselves, apprehended. The largeness of the plan upon which it was conceived involved the expenditure, year by year, of more money than any one of us, from Dr. Harper down, believed possible. This difficulty was inherent in the beginnings of the undertaking. The present year will close five years of our history. The University is now complete so far as it is essential to the President's plan. He, himself, has no thought of increasing the work of the institution beyond its present compass, except through the addition of two or three great departments by special contributions, such as Medicine, Law, and Technology.[50]

Harper was not insensitive to the problem of funding. In his ten-year report in 1902 he expressed the hope that professional education would become a priority, reflecting the quality of the existing graduate programs. He projected a financial need for $7,050,000: $500,000 for law, $4,550,000 for medicine, and $2,000,000 for technology. But the process of adding the professional schools to the university proper would not be an easy task for Harper.

The question of professional education first arose before the university officially opened, when it appeared that an estate would provide for a technical school to be affiliated with the institution. This project never materialized. One year later a trustee visited several European universities to gather material that would be helpful in recommending a design for a school of engineering. When Harper then pushed the trustees to move in the direction of these recommendations, the trustee himself countered: "Now! . . . where is the money to come from?"[51] Not one to be daunted by such considerations, Harper pursued an approach which would become a Harper tradition and which had a precedent in the eastern institutions: find another institution and annex it to the university. His first attempt, involving the Chicago Manual Training High School, met with great resistance from Frederick T. Gates, Rockefeller's representative. Harper also tried for many years to arrange an affiliation with the Armour Institute of Technology. Rockefeller continued to be unresponsive.[52]

The attempt to establish instruction in business met with greater success, largely due to the interest of J. Lawrence Laughlin, head of the political economy department. At the time business instruction in American education was available

only at the Wharton School in Philadelphia. Laughlin hoped
that the recommended College of Commerce and Administration would gain acceptance as a liberal art. With a motley
curriculum proposed, including journalism, business, diplo-
macy, law, and social service, the college was to educate students for business in a broad sense. In 1894 Laughlin urged
that a School of Commerce and Industrial Science emerge from
the old college to provide education as professional as that obtained in medical and law schools. The scheme as outlined in
1895 included political economy, economic history, public finance, constitutional law, international law, common law,
American and European history, and the sociology of society.[53]
Highly controversial and unacceptable to the University Senate, the college was nonetheless announced in 1898. Most
faculty viewed it as a step-child, and the scope of the instruction was never clearly defined.

Studies in pedagogy began in 1894 when John Dewey, head
professor of the Department of Philosophy, announced that a
fellowship would be available in pedagogy. One year later the
Department of Pedagogy was formally announced, with Dewey
as head professor. Dewey distinguished between efforts to train
teachers and efforts to train those who intended to be teachers
of teachers. His interest was in providing the latter with instruction and testing, emphasizing research in education. The
training of future teachers of teachers was to focus on philosophy and psychology as these disciplines related to pedagogical
research. "It is obvious, without argument," Dewey said, "that
this higher type of training must be undertaken for the most
part, if it is to be done in America at all, by the universities and
to a considerable extent as graduate work."[54] Thus Dewey
pioneered in establishing a program in the Department of
Education which was professionally oriented at the graduate
level. But Dewey's relation with Harper became strained. The
attempts to merge Dewey's laboratory school, which was
founded in 1896, into the official university structure were not
easy, and the financial problems were great. Dewey, frustrated
over numerous issues, finally left for Columbia.[55]

Yet Harper continued his attempts to establish professional
education in other areas that would not be part of the collegiate
curriculum but that would be solidly established as graduate

study. He turned to medicine and law. Always urging high standards, he rigorously denounced the conventional format of schools of medicine and law. Until these new programs could be done properly and financed sufficiently, the university would do without professional programs. On this issue there could be no compromise. As Goodspeed and others noted: "the great prepossession of his life was the development of the University in accordance with his conception of what it ought to be."[56] In his public statements from his earliest days as president, Harper spoke of the need for great schools of law and medicine, constantly lamenting the fact that they had yet to be born. "The professional schools with low requirements for admission attract many students who might otherwise take a College course. This multiplication of medical schools and law schools of a low grade is one of the greatest evils in connection with education work," Harper declared in a speech at Muskingum College. "It is an evil which seems to be increasing, and one which, in many sections of the country, is encouraged for political reasons by our legislators."[57]

Discussion about a medical school for the university was stimulated in 1894 by two developments: requests for affiliation from two schools and the beginning of Harper's correspondence with Rush Medical College. Harper was cautioned against considering seriously the requests for affiliation (his penchant for pursuing this kind of arrangement was known). One doctor urged him to move carefully, as "seductive propositions were made to Johns Hopkins University and resisted. Had they not been, she would not be in the vanguard of medical education in America."[58] Although affiliated with Lake Forest University, Rush Medical College pursued the negotiations. The university trustees insisted that Rush abandon its tradition of proprietary medicine and further that the Rush teaching faculty be replaced by men approved by the trustees in order to avoid conflicts of financial interests. Other requirements were stated: Rush was to pay off its debts, admission standards were to be raised, and the entire control of Rush was to change hands. Upon hearing the news of the trustees' approval of the affiliation, Rockefeller was silent. His displeasure could be glimpsed in the statements of his representative. "I have no doubt that Mr. Rockefeller would favor an institution that was neither allopath or homeopath but simply scientific in its investigation of medical science," Gates wrote to Goodspeed. "For that the University should wait and reserve the great weight of its influence, authority, and prestige instead of bestowing the same gratuitously on Rush Medical College."[59]

In announcing the new affiliation in 1898 Harper carefully noted that Rush was not to be considered the university's medical school. "Whether Rush Medical School will ever become the Medical School of the University, time will show."[60] The turn of the century still found the university without a medical school, and when discussions concerning Rush began anew in 1902 Rockefeller continued to show resistance.[61] The proponents for union with Rush cited the numerous changes at Rush which had enhanced the quality of medical education there since 1898: higher admission standards, examinations conducted by the university, creation of smaller sections, opportunity for election of courses during the latter years, establment of a library, student work in laboratories, and the transfer of preclinical instruction to the university, which amounted to half of the study conducted at the university.

Thus Harper's interest in professional education was evident in the earliest discussions of his university. In the case of law, schools like Northwestern and the Chicago College of Law would not serve as appropriate models. Proprietary operations characterized by minimal standards of education could not be tolerated in a university environment. Without the money necessary to establish a law school integral to the mission and life of the institution, Harper preferred to wait. Yet his commitment to professional education was strong, and indeed, as time would reveal, his notions of legal education and his ability to implement them were to have significant implications for higher education.

2   Early Discussions on Harper's Law School

Harper's First Thoughts
An Institute of Legal Research

In a handwritten note on the back of his first annual ledger, for 1891, Harper outlined his hopes for incorporating professional education into the university. His thoughts, hurriedly dashed off, would change significantly in the next several years. Titling his comments "Reciprocity," Harper discussed the relation of the university to the city and the established professions. "The City of Chicago is rapidly becoming a centre of educational influence. Already many professional schools have been established. The work of the professional school in whatever line, is more or less closely connected with that of the University."[1]

Yet in these notes Harper did not reveal any particulars for incorporating professional education in his design. The stance, characteristic of Harper's early thoughts on professional education as well as on traditions in American higher education, called for affiliation. Harper stated that students of the theological schools, law schools, and medical schools in the city of Chicago should "avail themselves of some of the opportunities of the University."[2] Yet in a short period of time members of the legal community, certain faculty, and several trustees influenced Harper greatly, and the idea of affiliation disappeared. A new concept of legal education emerged, one calling for the incorporation of professional education into the everyday life of the university.

Following a summer abroad during which he visited Oxford, Cambridge, Berlin, Leipzig, and the University of Paris, Harper prepared his first plan for the trustees in December of 1891. Harper had been impressed with the grander, more scholarly functions found in the continental universities, and his plan included the professional schools as an integral part of the academic life of the university. It is understandable that his interest in legal education would be well-received by the trustees. Five members of the initial board of twenty-one trustees were lawyers: Joseph M. Bailey, member of the State of Illinois Supreme Court and later chief justice; Eli B. Felsenthal, a lawyer and trustee of the old university; C. W. Needham, an active practitioner in Chicago; Daniel L. Shorey, a retired lawyer; and Frederick A. Smith, an alumnus of the old university who was a judge in the Chicago courts, and who served as second vice-president of the board. Later in the decade of the 1890s, as the discussions on legal education at Chicago continued, additional judges were added to the board: Jesse M. Baldwin, Franklin MacVeagh, Frank O. Lowden, J. Otis Humphrey, and Justice Charles Evans Hughes.

In his report for 1892 Harper again discussed the desirability of a law school in his plan of the university proper.[3] In 1893 the president of Columbian University in Washington, D.C., James C. Wellig, proposed that the University of Chicago take over his law school. Columbian, later to become George Washington University, was one of the institutions Rockefeller had considered supporting when he was courted by many institutions for his millions. Harper himself had had earlier connections with Columbian and indeed proposed in 1890 that Columbian be united with the University of Chicago. "I feel now that if this cannot be carried through, I do not care to go to Chicago."[4] Yet in 1893 he was unresponsive to the suggestion that the Columbian Law School become affiliated with the university.

Harper's vision of legal education began to assume grand proportions. His growing interest is revealed in a newspaper interview in 1893. Several objectives were expressed which would be heard often as his plans emerged. The school would not be a technical institution or a mere offshoot of a law office. To warrant its inclusion in the university proper, it was to be a school of jurisprudence and of jurists, with a curriculum devoted essentially to research and the higher study of law. In order to assure a high quality of professional education, the law students studying in this "institute of legal research" were to be college graduates, thus placing law study at the same level as graduate education. The law professors would be full-time faculty, not attorneys and judges on loan to the university.[5]

Harper turned to many sources for counsel in his design for a law school. In January 1893 he received a memorandum entitled "Memorial on the Creation of a Law School in the University of Chicago" from Thomas J. Lawrence.[6] Lawrence had strong opinions about the function of a law school, and many of these opinions differed markedly from the existing practices in American legal education. A university extension professor of history and international law for one year, Lawrence had received his A.B., LL.B., A.M., LL.M., and LL.D. degrees from Cambridge.[7] Except for an occasional leave, he had been in residence at Cambridge since 1872, first as student and then at various times as dean of Downing College, lecturer, tutor, warden of Cavendish College, and deputy professor of international law.

Unfortunately, we do not know how Harper met Lawrence or indeed if Harper had seen him during his visit to Cambridge. We do know that at this time in his career Lawrence was active as secretary and chairman of the Cambridge University Extension Lecturer's Union and was well-known as an advisor on technical education. In late 1891 Harper extended to him an appointment at the University of Chicago, and Lawrence responded in a lengthy letter on February 29, 1892. Lawrence indicated his interest in teaching courses on the growth of law and government, political philosophy, international law, constitutional law, and English history.

In regard to these subjects Lawrence indicated that they "are large subjects and would each take six months to deal with thoroughly. They can easily be divided into a number of smaller courses, e.g., The International Law of War, The International Law of Peace, The International Law of Neutrality, The Law of Maritime Capture, Leading Cases in International Law, Leading Cases in Constitutional Law."[8] Lawrence described his proposed university course on political philosophy as "a specimen of a course in Jurisprudence and Political Philosophy."

The four-page memorandum submitted by Lawrence in 1893 merits special note as many of the ideas presented in it ran counter to existing traditions. The memorandum proposed a school emphasizing legal research. The instruction was not to be limited to turning out technicians or even practicing attorneys. It "must aim at something more than the preparation of its students to practice. It must make legal studies into an instrument of liberal education. Unless they can be so used they have no place in the University *curriculum*." The issue which emerged concerned how extensively the principle of legal research was to permeate the program. Lawrence believed that the curriculum must adapt "to the wants of those who seek culture as well as professional knowledge. Such persons will desire to become acquainted with the history of their subject, with the scientific analysis of legal conceptions and with the ideals at which Law should aim, as well as with the technical rules which govern the cases that will come before them in their daily work."

Lawrence's final objective in teaching these students was elitist at a time when law schools were interested in turning out technicians to handle routine matters of law. In view of Harper's interest in turning out men and women who would assume major positions of responsibility in society, it is understandable how he was receptive to Lawrence's counsel that "it should be the object of the University of Chicago to give such students as these a training that will enable them to become leaders of the bar and ornaments of the bench, inspiring teachers, scientific writers and wise reformers, rather than to produce the greatest possible output of eager youths, quick to pick up professional technicalities and careless of aught beyond professional emolument."

The attainment of these lofty goals could be met, according to Lawrence, with courses on American public law, American private law, Roman law, international law, and jurisprudence. Lawrence detailed the proper sequence of the courses and urged Harper to consider a six-year program. Harper, who enjoyed tampering with the accepted college formats, undoubtedly noted this recommendation with particular interest.[9] The first two years would be in the academic college and the second two years in the university college where the student might take half of his courses in law "provided that he begin with comparatively simple subjects." Then, if the student wished to qualify for practice or obtain a legal degree, two years of additional study would lead to a master of laws (LL.M). Lawrence was reaching for a program that would combine college background and graduate study of the law. "No Chicago student would be admitted into the legal profession unless he had spent six years at the University." The sequence of courses "begins by rigidity, and ends by allowing the student a large choice of subjects which he can take in what order he pleases, as long as he does the proper amount of work each term and covers the whole ground in the appointed time." Lawrence suggested that some courses, like Roman law, international law, and constitutional law, might be optional but that others, like property, would be compulsory.

Finally Lawrence observed that at least five professors would be required: two professors of American law, one of Roman law and jurisprudence, one of American constitutional history, and one of international law and comparative politics. "The last two already exist," noted Lawrence, referring probably to Herman E. von Holst, whom Harper had enticed from the University of Freiberg as head professor of history and who had great interest in international politics, and Harry Pratt Judson, a distinguished professor of constitutional history and later Harper's successor as president of the university. Then in a concluding argument which must have been especially appreciated by Harper, who was financially beset from all sides, Lawrence maintained: "The other three can be obtained without any vast increase of expenditure. A School of Law does not require costly buildings and elaborate apparatus. It is equipped when a few lecture rooms, a good library, and a group of competent instructors are obtained. The Courts are its Laboratories, and they are provided at the public charge. Its material is human action and human passion, and these every community possesses in abundance."

The day after receiving Lawrence's "Memorial," Harper noted in a progress report that "instead of the two men of a year ago there are today at work 120. In estimating the number it should be remembered that no facilities of law and medicine have yet been organized."[10] In the next several years, as he waited for the money to become available, Harper was to refer often to his dream of legal education on the Midway. A year later, in 1893, at the fall convocation, Harper alluded to hopes for a law school but cautioned that money was needed before the plans could be realized.[11] In an address two days later Harper announced that the time had come to build a law school.[12] In his annual report in 1894 his commitment to a law school was expressed in terms of the first priority. "A question which is asked of us every day, and some days many times, concerns the organization of Schools of Medicine and Law. The only answer it has been possible to give to these many inquiries is that the University is wanting. It is taken for granted that the organization of an institution will not be complete until these schools have been established. But it is not possible to do all things at once."[13]

The financial pressures of sustaining the institution bore heavily on Harper, whose intent from the outset in creating the university was to do all things at once. "To establish a School of Jurisprudence and Law which should take high rank among the great schools of this country and of foreign countries will require the sum of one million dollars," Harper declared in his 1894 report. At a meeting of the University Senate on October 6, 1894, Harper told the faculty that there was a possibility of the organization of a law school the next October. The counsel of his advisors could readily be seen as the president concluded: "Our country has Law Schools and Medical Schools enough of the kind that are conducted without endowment and managed chiefly for the pecuniary or professional profit of those in charge of them. Rather than duplicate work that is already done, whether of high or low character, it would seem a better policy patiently to wait until broad-minded men who have at heart the cause of humanity shall see the opportunity to do something of which the whole world will be proud."[14]

Harper was not to be discouraged by the financial problems which dimmed the prospects for a law school on the Midway. Himself the author of a book on the legal literature of Babylon, he continued to look for the right design and the appropriate time for legal education to find its place in his university.

Harper and Freund
A School of Jurisprudence
or of Law?

An editorial in the university's *Weekly* on June 21, 1894, inquired whether the appointment of Ernst Freund to the Department of Political Science indicated that Harper had made a significant move in the establishment of a law school on the Midway.[15] Although there is no recorded response by Harper to the student newspaper's query, the answer was affirmative and would be demonstrated as the decade passed and Harper's law school came into being. Born in 1864 in New York City when his parents were visiting from Germany, Freund went to Germany and attended the Kreuzschule at Dresden and then the gymnasium in Frankfort-on-the-Main. Following graduation, he studied at the universities of Berlin and Heidelberg for four years, receiving a doctorate in canon and civil law from Heidelberg in 1884. He then returned to his birthplace and attended Columbia College for two years and practiced law from 1886 until 1894. While pursuing graduate work at Columbia in 1892 and 1893, he taught public law. After accepting Harper's invitation to join the political science faculty at Chicago, he taught Roman law, public law, and jurisprudence.[16]

From his earliest days on the Midway, Freund was Harper's major counsel in regard to the creation of a law school. Indeed Justice Felix Frankfurter, at the inaugural Ernst Freund Lecture, suggested that "Freund was the father of the Law School."[17] Freund did not favor the institute for legal research that was initially pressed upon Harper by Lawrence and others, even though he taught jurisprudence himself (his research in this area was to become essential to the establishment of administrative law in American legal education). As Justice Frankfurter noted: "He [Freund] was a pioneer in two domains which, until his coming, were nonexistent in our legal scholarship, namely administrative law and legislation. It was good fortune that Ernst Freund was educated abroad, so that he had drunk the best there was of German scholarship and was aware, just as Maitland had been aware fifty years earlier, of administrative law before it received a rubric and became the canon of our laws."[18]

Asked to give the convocation speech in June 1932 before the professional school graduates, as a last-minute substitute for the ailing Robert Maynard Hutchins, Freund spoke of the issues discussed extensively at the university during the nineties regarding the nature of legal education. He recalled that "there was quite a demand at the time that the school not be 'merely professional,' but should set itself up as a school of jurisprudence; but those who made the issue were not entirely clear as to its implications."[19]

As far as Freund was concerned, law was being taught at the university before the Law School opened in 1902. The State Board of Law Examiners recognized study done under Freund in the Department of Political Science and would certify one year's study if a student took at least six majors in the legal courses offered by the department and if three of the six were taken from the group entitled "Jurisprudence." In a discussion in which he referred to the teaching of Burgess, John Bassett Moore, Goodnow, and Munroe Smith, who all taught at Columbia's School of Political Science ("names that any law faculty would be glad to count among its own"), Freund declared that "when the University of Chicago was established, the greater part of this law work was introduced into the Department of Political Science, and was carried on for a number of years before there was a law school."[20]

Prior to meeting Freund, Harper had flirted seriously with the notion of an institute for legal research. But, according to Frederick Woodward, "Freund was instrumental in convincing him that the more urgent need was for a professional school of high standards and that emphasis on research would naturally develop in such an institution."[21] Freund himself modestly observed that "President Harper wisely concluded that the vital thing was the establishment of the highest professional standards, leaving the question of jurisprudence in abeyance."[22]

Yet the issue of whether the school should be one of jurisprudence or whether it should be a strictly professional school that would rival Harvard's was not one which Freund was to dismiss completely; his own interests played a major role in the shaping of Harper's law school. His position is perhaps best understood by examining the issues as Freund himself posed them:

> To my question: Is jurisprudence something better than law? Is scientific different from professional law? Should scientific law be merged in the social sciences? I suggest a demurrer rather than an answer. I do think that if we had established a school of jurisprudence we should have been disappointed in our expectations. . . . Unless within the limitations of time and equipment, a university law school explores all the resources of law, learns from history, and inspires itself by university ideals, it does not do its full duty to the legal profession; but if, inspired by these ideals, it succeeds in broadening and deepening the law-consciousness of the legal profession, and indirectly thereby of the community, that will also be the most valuable contribution that a university can make to law and to legal science.[23]

Harper continued to look to Freund for advice. On January 31, 1895, Freund submitted to the president an outline of a program of study, noting that he had "written the greater portion of the Law School circular, and expect to have it ready for you on Monday or Tuesday next."[24] The plans submitted by Freund laid out a curriculum differing from existing models, including those at Harvard and Columbia. He recommended professors from outside the university to conduct the instruction, several of whom were to play central roles in the formation of the school. Calling for a three-year program, Freund divided the curriculum into four areas: persons and property, commercial law, procedure, and public law. All first-year students would be required to take domestic relations, torts, criminal law, and property in the persons and property area; contracts in the commercial law area; common law pleading and procedure and practice in the procedure area; and constitutional law and international law in the public law area. But Freund's proposed curriculum was even more diverse than the traditional east coast models as reflected in the requirement of constitutional and international law for first-year students. It is important to note that public law at this time was a missing element in American legal education, at least as part of the regular curriculum, even at the best law schools. In regard to possible faculty, Freund reminded Harper that he had taught all of the courses noted in the persons and property curriculum but also recommended that Wigmore, then at Northwestern, might teach torts. Sensitive to Harper's well-established procedure of securing the best professors available in America, Freund suggested that Joseph H. Beale from Harvard might teach criminal law. In the public law area he suggested himself for constitutional law and Judson for international law.

The courses required for the second and third years included wills and conveyancing in the property area; sales and agency, bailments, debts, associations, and bankruptcy in the commercial area; and equity, evidence, and practice in the procedural area. He did not recommend any required courses in the public area. Again turning to major figures in legal education, Freund suggested that Wigmore or Beale could teach bailments; Judge Julian Mack, debts; Floyd Mechem, who was Tappan Professor at Michigan, associations; and Wigmore, evidence. He divided the elective courses for second- and third-year students into two areas: law and jurisprudence. In the area of law, students could elect admiralty, patents, insurance, U.S. Courts jurisdiction, damages, administrative law, municipal corporations, conflicts of laws, and federal constitutional law. In the area of jurisprudence, courses would be offered in criminology, relation of sales and industry, finance, railroad transportation, accounting, banking, experimental psychology, history of political ethics, comparative politics, the diplomatic history of the United States and Europe, municipal sociology, government of economics, and American political theory. Although sporadic attempts had been made elsewhere to offer constitutional law, the courses suggested by Freund were not included within law school curricula. The elective courses suggested by Freund in jurisprudence were also, for the most part, unheard of in legal education.

There are no documents to illuminate Harper's immediate response to Freund's proposed curriculum or to the suggested faculty members. Harper's hopes for the establishment of a law school increased despite the financial pressures he faced daily. He held regular conferences with members of the bar

and bench. On March 6, 1897, at the meeting of the University
Senate, a Committee on Higher Degrees appointed by Harper
recommended flexibility in awarding degrees for graduate
study. "Subsequent groups may be created," the committee
noted, "whenever schools of Law, Medicine, etc. may be added
to The University."[25] Several weeks later in an official statement to the university, Harper expressed concern over the
annual financial deficit but quickly expressed his hope that the
university would continue to grow. Citing the lack of funds,
he declared that the university would not "authorize payment
of a single dollar for which actual provision has not been
made," yet added, "it will be noticed that The University is
not yet able to offer instruction in law, in medicine or in technology."[26]

Counsel from the Bar

Turning outside the university for counsel concerning his proposed law school, Harper approached members of the Chicago
bar. On May 10, 1898, Adelbert Hamilton, a member of the
Chicago law firm of Hamilton and Stevenson and an instructor
at the Chicago College of Law, submitted a report to Harper
that had been "promised to you some time ago."[27] Copies of
the report—*Suggestions as to Organizing a Law Department
in the University of Chicago*—were printed for distribution,
although Hamilton required that the immediate distribution be
limited to Dr. Goodspeed: "I have refrained from placing them
at the disposal of other institutions than the University of
Chicago for whose use the work is intended. In this course even
my own school has not been excepted."[28]

Many of the themes already submitted to Harper by Freund
and Lawrence were reinforced in Hamilton's report. Referring
to the quality of the men necessary to constitute the faculty
that would teach the curriculum which he extensively outlined,
Hamilton cautioned Harper: "It will not be easy to secure, in
fact it will probably be impossible to secure in Chicago alone,
a faculty that can teach the outline of work I put before you;
especially the more advanced parts of it dealing with international, constitutional and administrative law and with com-

parative law, Roman law and legal history. Certainly there is no faculty organized here at present so as to do the work desired with thoroughness, ability and distinction."

A criticism of existing law schools and a call for excellence and innovation in professional legal education were the primary themes of Hamilton's thirty-two page statement. Noting the mediocre state of existing legal education, Hamilton concluded that "any one examining schemes of instruction in law schools of the United States will notice their diversity and planlessness. . . . In seven or eight years of law school work, no scheme of law study has been seen by the writer which could justly claim to be complete, well balanced, and thorough, to be arranged with reference to the science of jurisprudence and to be taught in an orderly, logical manner by approved, well applied methods of instruction."[29] Hamilton then elaborated five major fundamental ideas for Harper to keep in mind in the organization of, at least for Hamilton, a model law school.

Hamilton first called for a national school of law. "This character," he suggested, echoing President Charles W. Eliot at Harvard, "is essential to enable the department to assume rank in accordance with the dignity of the University." Moreover, a national school would draw students from all parts of the country. Enlarging Freund's arguments for a revision of the standard law school curriculum, Hamilton argued for extensions of the curriculum to cover the field of law as administered throughout the United States and for an avoidance of the curricula of parochial law schools. "These extensions are in the subjects of pleading and practice, civil or Roman law and federal law. At present no law school within my knowledge presents a scheme of instruction which if thoroughly studied will fit a student to practice according to any or all of the systems of procedure in vogue in the United States."[30] Criticizing prevalent practices that permitted automatic admission to the bar upon receipt of a law degree, Hamilton urged Harper to consider that a national law school should not be dependent upon any particular state and that students should be prepared to practice in any jurisdiction.

Hamilton's second fundamental premise was that most law school curricula were defective. In part Hamilton attributed the inadequate curricula to the lack of suitable books and to the fact that most professors were "practicing as distinguished from scientific lawyers." Hamilton discussed the defective areas in a manner fitting to a practicing lawyer. The first of these areas, suggested Hamilton, was the "art of practicing law. For example, in no less an institution than Harvard Law School the art of practice seems to be almost wholly neglected." In the second area Hamilton concurred with Freund that certain parts of the law were either not taught at all or were defectively taught because they had not been "hewn out of the rough materials of jurisprudence and erected into a clear, well defined body of elementary law suitable to be taught." He then cited the subject of administrative law and the law of remedies.[31]

The third premise presented by Hamilton concerned the method of instruction. He was not willing to accept any of the three current methods of instruction as the proper one: the textbook method, lectures, or the case method. For Hamilton each method had advantages and disadvantages. He counseled Harper to adopt all those methods, taking care "to use them in their appropriate places with a view of producing the best results with the greatest reasonable economy of time and labor." The textbook method might present the law as a comprehensible whole but encourages a "memory-operation" by the student. The case method, suggested Hamilton, might supplement the textbook method by "disciplining the mind to analyze legal problems and to apply to conditions of facts their appropriate legal principles." Yet it was a slow method, and students were not able to study an adequate number of cases for a comprehensive "thorough grasp of the law in its entirety."[32] For Hamilton lectures were necessary because of the lack of proper books.

Hamilton urged Harper to appoint faculty who would give their time exclusively to teaching law, particularly in the substantive areas of the law. In the areas of adjective law, defined by Hamilton as the "law of the methods by which rights are asserted," which included remedies, pleading, evidence, practice, and procedure, judges and lawyers should be utilized. Hamilton then made a strong case for the inclusion of practicing lawyers on the faculty:

If I may venture criticism of so admirable an institution
as Harvard Law School it is that since the days when Story,
Greenleaf and Washburn were connected with the school
it has lost touch with great leaders among jurists and
lawyers. I believe this loss is real and that as between two
law schools one like Harvard, where nine of the ten men in
the faculty give their time exclusively to teaching law, and
another school where instruction is in charge of persons
exclusively teaching law but whose work is supplemented by
that of an able corps of instructors drawn from the bench
and from the ranks of active practitioners, students may well
prefer the latter institution. If well selected such men give
distinction to a school.[33]

The final fundamental principle suggested to Harper was
that students should give their entire time to the study of law.
"The reason for this requirement is because of the magnitude
and difficulties of the task of mastering the legal field." A student could not learn the law, Hamilton maintained, merely by
reading and reciting it. The "law must be applied to actual legal
problems." A student attending a law school must see it as a
full-time business. "That proverbial jealousy accredited to the
law as a mistress is as applicable to the student as to the lawyer in practice."[34]

Hamilton's outline of study formed the largest part of his
recommendations to Harper. The general scheme was to move
from the general to the particular. The student was to be first
introduced to the elements of law, also called jurisprudence,
which was defined by Hamilton as "the science which reduces
legal phenomena to order and coherence. In this sense jurisprudence stands to the law in much the same relation that
grammar does to language." This introduction included "the
three great subjects, international law, public law, and private
law." Subjects included elements of jurisprudence, international persons and rights, constitutional law, administrative
law, and traditional substantive law. This survey, suggested
Hamilton, would take four months and should be taught by
recitations from the books that he listed.

The next level of instruction used "an elementary analysis
calculated to familiarize the student with the principal topics

of law, its nomenclature, definitions and principles." The subjects noted above were expanded, to be taught by a combination of recitation and casework over a twelve-month period. The emphasis was on substantive law, and Hamilton insisted on an orderly method for the study of law. The principles of constitutional law must be taught before property, personal rights, contracts, and the like were studied. Thus the subjects were arranged so as "to make a principal matter precede in study one that is dependent on it."[35]

The next department of study presented by Hamilton was advanced adjective law. By means of a combination of recitation and casework over a twelve-month period, the students would be trained in "the science and arts of general practice, and special work." Although textbooks would be used during this period, "fully two-thirds of the work demands the actual drafting of documents and the study of cases and statutes, the student using the case method and the instructor lecturing. This is both desirable and necessary."[36] But, like Freund, Hamilton never departed from his insistence that the "three great subjects of international law, public law, and private law" be part of the curriculum. Indeed he insisted that students be required to take international law and public law throughout the twenty-seven-month curriculum (nine months of work in each of three years). Upon completion of the program the LL.B. degree would be awarded.

Apparently not satisfied that his three-year design for a model law school was thoroughly comprehensive, Hamilton then outlined for Harper a master's program. Acknowledging that the primary purpose of a law school was "to prepare men for the general practice of law," Hamilton continued: "but besides men who simply desire to be fitted for practice there are others whose time, means and disposition render a more scholarly preparation both possible and desirable."[37] He expanded the "three great subjects to include Roman law, continental European and Spanish-American law, legal history, and social economics. "The preparation of men for the Master's degree may be said to be the second purpose of a well organized law school's course of instruction. A third purpose is the fitting of men who desire to enter upon the pursuit of some branch or department of practice." For such lawyers, Hamilton proposed special courses in admiralty, banking, corporation, mining, patent, and railway law. Nine months of study would be necessary for an advanced degree.

The culmination of legal study for Hamilton, as expressed in his proposed curriculum, was social economics, or principles of statesmanship, "believed to be unique in law school curricula." For Hamilton this course was a natural outgrowth of the study of law:

> The development of law is in one way always a crystallization into customary rules or statutory enactments of economics and social principles which are themselves in a constant state of development with the progress of civilization. The course in the principles of statesmanship contemplates a definition of social progress and its laws, a thorough grounding in the principles of economic production and distribution, and an exposition of the principles of practical statesmanship, which shall unfold the meaning of the doctrines of *Laissez Faire* and protection, define the nature and functions of the state, formulate the principles of international trade and of economic taxation, show the relation of the state to the development of industrial organizations, and indicate the correlation of the law with the principles of sociology so far as the latter have been worked out.[38]

Citing the Harvard course of instruction for 1897–98, Hamilton voiced four criticisms of this traditional model. First, the "Harvard course is not correlated to any jurisprudential scheme." Hamilton substantiated his opinion by observing that no criteria existed to determine whether the Harvard course was complete or logically arranged. His greatest objection to the Harvard model was the exclusive adherence to the case method. Because of the slowness of this method Hamilton could not see how the field of law, as he outlined it, could be covered in three years. Furthermore, Hamilton insisted to Harper, the "Harvard course is defective: the use of the case method involves the sacrifice of the great topics of international law and of public law during the first and second years except in the single topic of criminal law and procedure. . . . Jurisprudence in the sense of legal grammar, an elementary study of the greatest importance to law students, is likewise omitted." Finally, he argued that the Harvard course was "without reference to any logical correlation of subjects." He supported this argument by citing the fact that constitutional law, a field in which fundamental principles could be identified and taught, was not presented until the third year.[39]

Hamilton's conclusion to his suggestions to Harper in May of 1898 were eloquent and must have been well received by Harper. The rhetoric might well have been Harper's, and indeed the opinions that Hamilton expressed would become increasingly evident in Harper's own statements. For Hamilton a law school, if it was a national one, was the most important part of a university. "It may send forth men who become notable in art, literature, science and philosophy. Its seminaries may graduate others who become eminent as divines. Its schools of medicine may educate skillful physicians and surgeons. But it is from the law schools that will come the accomplished lawyers, learned jurists and distinguished statesmen whose achievements will indicate most surely the worth of its privileges and shed most brilliant luster upon the character of the University."[40]

If properly designed, a national law school would open doors in all fields of industrial, commercial, professional, and public activities. The opportunity was great for the university to establish a new school, maintained Hamilton, because it "is in a position to begin this work absolutely fresh, untrammeled by unsuccessful attempts, unrestrained by the prejudices or policies of older institutions and with the support of a people whose liberality is never stinted where they are satisfied that an educational institution is founded upon lines of culture, deep, broad, and far-reaching in purposes of use, worth and beneficence."[41]

Although Hamilton placed a greater emphasis on the practical aspects of legal education than had Lawrence and Freund, the counsel of all three to Harper had much in common: the design of a graduate-level program, the need for a national law school, the desirability of full-time faculty, and, most significantly, a broadening of the curriculum to include areas outside of the traditional law courses and public law. Their insistence on a thorough examination and revitalization of the curriculum cannot be overemphasized.

Concerned over numerous obstacles, including the perpetual problem of money, negotiations with Rockefeller, and the question of a medical school, Harper was silent for several months about his hopes for a law school. However on April 1, 1899, in an official statement, Harper again lamented the absence of professional schools and reminded his audience that "the work of the University of Chicago should be rounded out, its faculties increased to include all of the work legitimately belonging to a university. The University has today, strictly speaking only two faculties, the Faculty of Divinity, and the Faculty of Arts and Science. There is no Faculty of Law, no Faculty of Medicine, no Faculty of Technology, or Engineering."[42] Harper continued by stating that the opportunities for greatness for the university would be increased with the addition of these faculties and noted that the work of many of the existing departments was already related to the proposed role of the professional schools and that as a result their establishment would be a natural growth.

"The question has many times been asked," said Harper, "Why did not the University undertake this professional work? The answer is simple enough. It seemed wiser not to spread out but rather to concentrate the income at our disposal upon that which the professional work might later be built."[43] There were many people, including Rockefeller, who felt that Harper had already done this in his attempt to build a great university overnight. But Harper was anxious to complete his vision and ready to move forward: it was only a question of time and money. The basic ideas and arguments for his law school had been presented.

3   Harper Expands the Role of University Legal Education

As Harper persistently sought advice concerning the possibilities of legal education, financial circumstances thwarted his hopes for the opening of a law school as the decade drew to a close. Freund, Lawrence, and Hamilton had suggested principles concerning the nature of legal education that were essential when Harper was finally able to establish a school: legal education was to embody professional, graduate-level instruction of the highest quality; students with a college background would be preferred for admission; instruction was to be given by full-time faculty; and there was to be no single method of instruction. Perhaps of greatest consequence was the insistence that the Harvard curriculum, considered the most advanced of the time, was not necessarily adequate and should not be transplanted from Cambridge to Chicago without thorough examination.

As Harper waited for the necessary funds and trustee approval for the opening of a law school, he continued to turn to others for advice and support. Encouraged by the success resulting from the arrangements concerning a medical school in 1900, Harper renewed his drive for trustee support and approval. Carefully considering the effect a law school would have on university life, he spoke on the need for making such a school an organic part of the whole university. In the spring of 1901, when he sensed that the time was right to move, he turned once more to Freund for counsel. In drawing up plans, Freund suggested again that Harper approach Harvard. The story of the negotiations between the two institutions is revealing. With vigor Harper tackled the project, armed with strong opinions on legal education and dedicated to establishing a law school which would surpass its Harvard progenitor.

48

Law: An Appendage or an Organic Part of the University?

"You have got the doctors, now Doctor Harper, get the lawyers, or you will be like a bird with only one wing. The University itself is a splendid body; the medics make an admirable left wing; now put on the right. It will be a great 'go'."[1] This advice, submitted on July 5, 1900, by Judge C. C. Kohlsaat, a distinguished member of the Chicago bar, was well received by Harper. Having worked out arrangements for a medical school, Harper was anxious to develop the university along lines that would be consistent with his conception of a new university. Unquestionably Harper was a promoter and wanted strong wings for his university. Yet the main thrust of his effort was to create an institution different from any existing in American higher education. Throughout the history of the founding of the Law School one can see the differences that resulted from Harper's emphasis on graduate training and his notion of a university in which the law school would be genuinely an organic part, not a self-supporting, autonomous professional school. This tension was evident prior to 1900 in the discussions of whether legal education at Chicago should be organized as an institute for jurisprudence or as a law school emulating the best models available in America. How would a law school fit into the scheme of a university that regarded itself as a new type of institution?

Judge Kohlsaat's counsel to Harper reflected the pressure on Harper from the organized bar for the creation of a law school. For Judge Kohlsaat, the model to be imitated at Chicago was Harvard: "There is another thing that I have been waiting to talk to you about, and that is the growing need of this community for a law school like that of Harvard. There is very great demand for it under the auspices of an educational institution like the University of Chicago." The judge, who had been active in the affairs of the Union College of Law, did not want to duplicate the programs of any of the local law schools. Critical of the proprietary schools, he noted that "we have a number of what I shall call 'cheap institutions,' and it is my judgment that the University could come very near to absorbing them all."[2]

Judge Kohlsaat's criticism of the existing legal education in Chicago was explicit. "I understand that the schools here now purport to be branches of one college or another; but they are so only in name, being run solely by the professors—planted by them and the fees harvested by them. The law school which shall succeed must be as much a part of the University in fact, as any of your courses. It should be run upon educational principles and not merely for tuition money, and be as much under the control and management of the President as in any department of the University."[3] Harper, in agreement with the judge's opinions, presented the communication to the trustees for their consideration the next month.

Closely associated with the pressure of the bar was a strong regional interest in the discussions about a law school. Thus in an official statement at a university convocation, Harper observed: "The members of the bar in this city have often taken occasion to express the opinion that there was a place in the city of Chicago and the West for a school of law, to which should be admitted only those who had finished a college course, or at least three years of such a course."[4] The assumption underlying the regional interest was that the standards of legal education as well as of higher education were inferior in the West to those in the East. Therefore Harper's university might make a significant regional contribution by any improvement over existing educational practice. This challenge was perhaps the greatest motivation for Harper as he elaborated his scheme, and the emphasis is clearly evident in his constant press for high-quality graduate education. Although undergraduate education was to play an important role in the university, Harper was more interested in the creation of a graduate institution. His conception of the university was a hybrid that combined features of the English system, the continental universities (the German university in particular), and the New England college.

Judge Kohlsaat urged that the law school be an integral part of the university, not an appendage to it. For Harper the notion of the wholeness of the institution was critical. As universities sprang up following the Civil War, their colleges or departments were loosely related to each other, if at all. In the East, universities grew out of the prestigious, well-established colleges which zealously guarded their autonomy and which viewed with trepidation the alteration of the collegiate tradition as graduate and professional programs evolved. These relations between departments and schools were what Harper considered "connections," not organic parts of a whole: "For a considerable time the tendency had been in the United States toward a connection between colleges or universities and law schools, but this connection did not involve any organic relation."[5] William S. Pattee observed different qualities in the rapidly rising institutions in the West:

> But when we turn our eyes to the Western States, we behold colleges and universities which seem to have sprung into existence by some magic influence. In the extent of their buildings and appointments generally, in the number of their students, in the vigor of their management, and in the thoroughness and inspiration of their instruction, they demonstrate their power to meet the demands of a vigorous and earnest people whose civilization and culture are but those of the East planted upon the broad prairies of the West, though intensified and broadened by the active and liberal spirit incident to a new country.[6]

As in the East, these new universities were loosely organized, with programs connected often only by the name of the institution. Professional schools in particular were usually spiritually, and often physically, alienated from the mainstream of an institution. In Harper's grand design, such a situation was not permissible. Harper organized the educational plan of the university in great detail, much to the chagrin of some.[7] Initially he had used the departmental structure which, although easy to administer, resulted in autonomous units. But as sharp lines of separation occurred in the mid 1890s, he became more concerned about the correlation of academic disciplines and about the relations among departments:

> The work of the student in the future will not be cut off into departments; on the contrary it will be the study of problems which will lead him into and through many departments of study. The need of correlation does not receive from most of us the appreciation which it deserves.

Our work as an institution will secure that unity of purpose
and the unity of result which are in the highest sense
desirable only in proportion as each department works in
the interest, not merely of itself, but also of its sister
departments.[8]

In June of 1901 the university sponsored a conference on
education. One of the major speakers, President George E.
MacLean of the State University of Iowa, addressed university
faculty and students on "The Relation of Professional Schools
to College Work." "The size of our problem appalls," observed
MacLean, whose comments were recorded in the University
Record. He noted the growth in the United States from two
professional schools in 1776 to 532 schools in 1901, with 10,029
instructors and 55,669 students. From 1888 to 1899 the number of professional students had increased 24 percent in theology, 224 percent in law, and 84 percent in medicine. Although
he acknowledged that many people within the professions
would view the increases with alarm, "in reality it marks extraordinary progress, because in this decade restrictive legislation has flourished and the terms of admission and graduation have advanced." With due respect for his audience, he
noted that "imperial Illinois leads for the first time in professional students with her 7,231 in 1899, but her pride is moder-
ated in comparison with other states by the lack of proper
control of the power to grant degrees and licenses."[9]

MacLean elaborated on attempts "to secure organic university relations and supervision." To document the argument he
observed that 138 professional schools in 1899 were separate
institutions and 229 were departments of colleges and universities. His assumption was that professional schools under
university supervision would have more rigorous standards.
If one were to look at even the best university law schools in
1899 this premise was questionable. A well-known Harvard
anecdote told by President Eliot recalled his first visit to the
Law School soon after his inauguration and the reaction of the
venerable Professor Washburn upon seeing Eliot enter his
classroom: "This is the first time," Washburn observed wryly,
"that I have ever seen a president of Harvard College in the
Law School."[10] The tradition in American legal education

called for autonomy and the creation of fiefdoms. Dwight's law school at Columbia was firmly established as his private property.

Any real connection between the law schools and their mother institutions had just begun toward the end of the century, as noted by Joseph H. Beale in his address on "The Place of Professional Education in the Universities."[11] Harper was in full sympathy with MacLean's opinion that "the professional school should be elevated in *name* as well as fact to a college in organic relation as part of the University." The professional school on the Continent historically had been a university college. Acknowledging that the notion of a college of arts as preparatory for a professional school might be "repugnant to the provincial modern," MacLean urged that the "college of liberal arts and the professional colleges should be connected organically, so that, in addition to the common life and privileges, students may pass from one to the other, and be put upon a level as to requirements for admission."[12]

As the discussions of the Law School continued, a constant theme would be the organic relationship between the school and the university. In drafting the first circular of information for the school, Freund highlighted this relationship in the introductory statement: "In addition to the interaction between law students and faculty, and the organization of law clubs for the argument and decision of questions of law," it "is also hoped that the students of the Law School will derive benefit from intercourse and interchange of thought with the other members of the student body of the University, of which they will form part." In the description of post-graduate study of law, Freund asserted that the work would be "closely affiliated with the work of the Departments of History, Political Economy, Political Science, and Sociology." Moreover the courses in the college and the schools of art, literature, and science would be available for law students without charge.[13]

In presenting his recommendations to the trustees for the establishment of the school, Harper's first point emphasized that legal education was to be integral to university life: "[the Law School] shall be located at the University, and thus constitute a part of the University environment and form an organic part of the University, making contribution to the

University life and at the same time imbibing the spirit and purpose of that life."[14]

Freund to Harper:
Turn to Harvard

Harper's talks with lawyers and judges in the spring of 1901 resulted in continued pressure from the bar and furthered his long-standing hope for the establishment of a law school. Writing on April 24 to his counselor, Ernst Freund, Harper asked for help: "I find there is a very strong feeling in the Board of Trustees that we ought to move pretty soon in the matter of a law school. I am wondering whether we could make a start in some such way as the medical school is starting."[15] Freund's response came the same day. "I am greatly interested to learn that the question of the law school is to be taken up. I shall be very happy to place my services at your disposal at any time that you may command them."[16] Unfortunately Harper was unable to move as quickly as he wanted. "When I get through with an attack of la grippe, with which I am now struggling, I should like to talk the matter over with you."[17] Often plagued by illness or simply fatigue, Harper was forced to lessen his hectic pace for several months.

Discussions between Freund and Harper, however, continued. In anticipation of a trip to New York City in December, Harper asked Freund for names of possible faculty as well as people in New York with whom he should talk regarding the nature of the proposed school. Freund's response helped in the establishment of the relation between Harvard and Chicago that would prove central to the definition of legal education at Chicago; it also created further tension between conflicting opinions as to what the structure of the new school would be. "The men whom I had above all in mind are Joseph H. Beale, Jr., and Ernest W. Huffcutt. The former is at Harvard, the latter at Cornell."[18] While noting that neither man could be seen by Harper in New York, Freund urged the president to talk with William A. Keener and George W. Kirchwey at Columbia Law School in regard to other names.[19] Freund continued by telling Harper: "it is extremely desirable that you should at some time have a talk with Professor James Barr Ames of the Harvard Law School, or should write to him. He could probably give you more information than anybody else about young men of promise who are qualified to teach law, and his general ideas on a law school would be most valuable."[20]

With his letter Freund submitted a list of nineteen possible faculty members, beginning with Beale. The first five men were major figures in legal education, and Freund briefly assessed each: Ernest W. Huffcutt, professor at Cornell University, "author of treatises on Agency and Negotiable Instruments, Harvard graduate, a student of high standing at the law school"; Melville M. Bigelow from Boston University Law School, "author of works in English legal history and of a number of legal textbooks (Torts, Bills and Notes, Estoppel, Fraud)"; Charles N. Gregory, formerly dean of Wisconsin Law School, currently at Iowa; and John H. Wigmore, dean of Northwestern Law School, "one of the most scholarly men among the law teachers of the country, highly spoken of by the students." The fifth man was Beale, who, according to Freund's summary to Harper, "has published collections of cases on Criminal Law and on Conflict of Laws; well-known as a law teacher, and highly spoken of by the students; said to be a man of executive ability." Freund also urged Harper to raid the Northwestern law faculty for three men in addition to Dean Wigmore: Blewett Lee, Julian W. Mack ("regarded by the students as the best teacher at Northwestern, Harvard Law School prize scholar"), and Charles C. Hyde, an alumnus of Harvard.[21]

Harper took Freund's counsel seriously. Several of the men suggested were to become central in the founding of Harper's law school; the man of immediate interest to the president would be Joseph Henry Beale, Jr. Although the story of the Harvard-Chicago relation and its effect on the organization of the Law School has been sketched elsewhere, it deserves more thorough examination.[22]

Freund's first choice, Joseph H. Beale, was forty years old and a professor of law at Harvard. Raised in Brahmin Boston, Beale attended Chauncy Hall School and was graduated from

Harvard College in 1882.[23] One of his colleagues, Samuel Williston, later observed that Beale "was early recognized as one of the most brilliant students in a class that contained half a dozen future Harvard professors besides a number of other men who in later life won distinction for scholarly achievement."[24] He taught for one year at St. Paul's School and returned to Harvard to study classics and history for one year. He then entered Harvard Law School and received his LL.B. and A.M. in 1887. He shared the leadership of his class with Julian Mack, the two thus beginning a close friendship which would last throughout their lives.[25] During their third year in law school Beale and Mack felt that their law work in the Thayer Club was not sufficient for their extracurricular interests. They and several others pulled together some student-written essays and proceeded to found the *Harvard Law Review*. Beale's article on "Tickets," which appeared in the first issue, is of particular interest since it was, as Samuel Williston noted, "wholly outside the somewhat restricted curriculum of the School at that time, and the keen and thorough treatment of the subject were characteristic of him."[26]

Upon graduation Beale, anxious to begin private practice, turned down the prestigious offer to serve as a secretary to Justice Horace Gray of the United States Supreme Court. From 1887 to 1897 he practiced law and was active in the affairs of Christ Church and in politics. In 1898 he was appointed by the governor to serve as a member of the Massachusetts Commission for the Simplification of Criminal Pleadings and helped draft the bill ultimately passed in 1899.[27] As a legal scholar, Beale had impeccable credentials. A frequent contributor to the *Harvard Law Review* and the *Green Bag*, he edited *Sedgwick on Damages*, May's *Criminal Law*, and Parson's *Partnership*. In addition to authoring a book on *Criminal Pleading and Practice*, Beale compiled casebooks on criminal law, carriers, damages, and conflict of laws. Active in the American Bar Association, he was a frequent speaker before legal and civic groups. He was later involved in the formation of the American Association of Law Schools and served as its president in 1914. But perhaps of greatest interest to Harper, who needed a man to serve as dean of his new school, Beale was a Harvard man —a product and representative of the greatest law school in

America.[28] If the question was which school would provide the best model to imitate, the choice for Harper was simple: he turned to Cambridge.

Harper Awaits Approval
to Move Ahead

Having received Freund's suggestions in December, 1901, Harper wanted to move quickly with his plans for the Law School as the winter quarter began. On January 9, 1902, he wrote to Freund, instructing him to put together a circular in order to have an outline for submission to the University Senate. "I think it is practically settled that we should have the school of law," Harper observed. "I would like to suggest that you undertake to prepare the first circular of information, modeling it in all aspects according to other circulars, bringing it into line with the University publications, putting into it all that is necessary for the student to know, but of course making it as brief as possible."[29] Harper suggested that Freund leave the faculty section blank. Harper's only other instruction called for a preliminary law year, which would be the first year of the senior college. Having made this request of Freund, Harper turned to Cambridge and the other task at hand: the question of the desirability of establishing a school like the Harvard Law School on the Midway.

The task would not prove to be a simple one. Harper entered negotiations with the Harvard Corporation for the loan of Beale to Chicago, even though Harper still had unsettled questions in his mind concerning the nature of legal education. His earliest vision of legal education had called for an institute of jurisprudence as opposed to the conventional university law school and, certainly, to the proprietary and independent schools of the period. Judge Kohlsaat and other trustees questioned whether the Harvard model should be used just as it stood. Again, the question was whether the law school should be an appendage to the institution, as at Harvard, or somehow be organically integrated into the expanding university. Conflicting opinions on these issues confronted Harper from many sources outside the university and, as he would soon discover, from Freund and Beale. Galusha Anderson, his close friend at whose home in Morgan Park he often stayed when he was ill, strongly urged Harper to be selective in taking ideas from Harvard. Anderson, a head professor in the divinity faculty, wrote to Harper to suggest Floyd Russell Mechem for the faculty: "he is the most forceful inspiring teacher that they have in the Law School at Ann Arbor." At the same time Anderson cautioned Harper that "it strikes me that it would not be best to reproduce the Harvard Law School here; we want what is good in Harvard, but our law school should be fitted to its environment."[30]

The case submitted by Anderson was grounded in the perceived need for practical legal education—a premise understandable when viewed from the vantage point of one who had been on the old University of Chicago Law Department faculty: "Most of the States have code practice, but we here in Illinois have the English Common law practice. Harvard is theoretical, doctrinaire, and should not have the privilege of just putting down its counterpart here; we are more practical and direct and all the better for that, and the practical direct element ought to find a large place in molding at the very start [of] our Law School."[31]

If Harper was uncertain about the proper format for the teaching of law, one must remember, as Edward H. Levi suggests, that "probably law, as a subject, was genuine and quite different for Harper who was a teacher, in some sense, of Old Testament law."[32] Thus it is understandable that Harper's approach to the study of law would be different from the approach used by the prevailing traditions. Yet as president of a university, he could not ignore the programs at universities he was trying to surpass. Harper's university had been conceived of as a place for discovery, investigation, and systematization of ideas. How would the study of law fit into this conception?

Although he was concerned with the definition of legal education, Harper moved energetically ahead to obtain Beale on loan and to organize a school. By means of a Senate Committee on Instruction and Equipment, consisting of Harry Pratt Judson, Albion W. Small, J. Laurence Laughlin, and Harper, a report was presented to the Board of Trustees on January 21, 1902, thirty days after Harper asked Freund to prepare a circular. The argument for the establishment of the Law School was based on several points. First was the necessity "to proceed to the organization of those departments of the University not yet established." The second argument was financial: the school should be self-supporting and thus not prove a drain on the limited resources of the university. Mention was made of the increased desire of men to study law and the fact that the university was presently giving the instruction that was called for in the Law School's first year. "The instruction called for in the remaining two years, the cost of administration, [and] the cost of advertising, etc., can be provided for a sum not to exceed $18,000 a year, and this expense would probably be met by the tuition fees of the students registering for the work."[33]

The committee noted that temporary quarters for the school could be arranged in the building then occupied by the Department of Education. The problem, at least as expressed in the report, concerned the necessity for providing a law library, estimated to cost $50,000. To resolve this problem the trustees voted to turn to Rockefeller, as they had done often before, and request the money. Interestingly, the initial recommendation submitted to the trustees at their January 21 meeting was prepared to read as follows: "That Mr. Rockefeller be requested to consider the advisability of giving to the University the sum of $50,000 for the purchase of a law library, and, if he shall consent, or, if not, and if the money can be obtained from any other source. . . ." At some point, either before the meeting, perhaps by Harper himself, or during the meeting, the words "or, if not, and if the money can be obtained from any other source," were crossed out with a pencil.[34] One can only speculate as to why the options for the financial support necessary to establish the school were limited to one. Perhaps Harper already had an indication of Rockefeller's interest. It is more likely, in view of Harper's bold way of negotiating with Rockefeller, that Harper chose to take the risk of a negative response.

The report of the Senate Committee on Instruction and Equipment was submitted to the board on January 21 and approved on March 14. Harper did not wait for the official authorization on March 14 and proceeded immediately after the January 21 meeting with the planning as sketched briefly in the committee's report: he assumed a positive answer from Rockefeller, with the receipt of $50,000 for the purchase of a law library and the approval of the founder for the establishment of a school of law. As usual his instincts were correct, and on March 14 Harper was authorized by the trustees to proceed with the organization of the University School of Law, to be open for instruction October 1, 1902.

Certain understandings were outlined by the trustees. Sensitive to the traditional annual deficits, the trustees specified that the total expense for the school, excluding the cost of the library, for the first year was not to exceed $18,000, and for the second year $22,000—"a sum estimated to correspond to the receipts from tuition fees and matriculation." The trustees called for an arrangement to include a preparatory year equivalent to the third college year, an opinion reflecting Harper's directive to Freund in the preparation of a tentative prelaw program on April 24, 1901. The trustees made it clear that the school was to be the equivalent of a graduate school, specifying "a three-year course of study, to which no one shall be admitted who is not a graduate of an approved college or who has not completed three years of study in such a college."[35]

Three fundamental points in regard to the policy of the School of Law were considered by both the Senate Committee on Instruction and Equipment and the trustees. On the first two points there was unanimity. The first has already been discussed: the insistence that the school "form an organic part of the University, making contribution to the University life and at the same time imbibing the spirit and purpose of that life." The second had already been hinted at in the approval of the Senate and the trustees of a three-year course of study: "that it should be essentially a graduate school, its regular students being required to have the Bachelor's degree, or at least three years of work in an approved college."[36]

But on the third fundamental, the desirability of utilizing exclusively the case method of instruction, the records show that "the feeling was not so unanimous." Having just approved the understanding that Harper should secure "the consent of the Harvard Corporation to grant Professor Beale leave of absence for two years to act as Dean of the new Law School during its period of organization," the trustees wavered when they voted: "while the methods of each instructor should be left to be determined by himself, the system which should serve as a basis of the work should be the so-called 'Case system.' "[37] Thus a basic problem was soon to become locked into the organizational efforts of the school. The view of the Harvard Corporation regarding Professor Beale's mission in Chicago was clear: "Voted that leave of absence without salary be granted to Professor J. H. Beale, Jr., from September 15, 1902, to February 15, 1903, provided that the School to be established at Chicago is to have ideals and methods similar to those of the Harvard Law School."[38]

Harper's uncertainty as to the nature of the program in law is reflected again at the March 14 meeting of the board, as the trustees voted their official approval of the recommendations for organization submitted to them by the Senate Committee at their January meeting. Harper suggested to the board that "Joseph Henry Beale, Jr. be appointed as Professor of Law in the School of Jurisprudence and Dean of the School." He did not suggest that the school be a law school but a school of jurisprudence.[39] The question of whether the law school was to be a wing of the university or an organic part of the whole still appeared moot despite Harper's rhetoric. Beale had yet to come to Chicago to begin his task of replicating the Harvard Law School. He had yet to confront Freund, who, like Harper, was to maintain strong notions on the nature of legal education that conflicted with basic principles at Harvard.

Harper Turns to Harvard
"Come Over into Macedonia
and Help Us"

Harper waited for official word from Rockefeller following the January meeting in 1902 of the trustees. Without the founder's financial support for a law library, Harper could only assume that his plans for expanding the university to encompass professional education were meeting with Rockefeller's displeasure, as had been the case in the attempts to establish a medical school, technological education, and a graduate program in education. In his statement at the winter convocation, Harper devoted a large portion of his discussion to the plans for the school, without alluding to the Harvard negotiations: "Many times each week, and almost every day, we are asked the question: Is it not possible for the University to establish a school of law and jurisprudence?" Speaking about the financial situation, Harper as fund-raiser insisted that a school of law would not require as large an endowment as that necessary for a school of technology or medicine. Indeed, he noted that only $500,000 would be necessary, as opposed to $5,000,000 for either of the other schools. "Perhaps," Harper said coyly, "the friends of the University might be willing to contribute $30,000 to $50,000 for the purchase of books absolutely required."[40]

Harper, increasingly impatient, came out strongly for immediate support:

> In any case, the question is one for serious consideration; and again, I may suggest, an opportunity is presented which perhaps someone will see fit to accept—the opportunity of cooperation with the University in a piece of work which is universally conceded to be necessary, and which with every year becomes more pressing.[41]

He did not have to wait long. The response from the founder occurred within thirty days of the trustee meeting. The letter from John D. Rockefeller, Jr., to Andrew McLeish, vice-president of the trustees, was strictly business. No reference was made to the structure or program of the proposed law school: "My father authorizes the expenditure of fifty thousand dollars ($50,000) for the purchase of a Law Library and the organization of a University School of Law as recommended by the Board, understanding that the total expense of the School, not including the cost of the library, for the first year shall not exceeed $18,000 and for the second year $22,000, a sum which it is estimated that the receipts from student fees and matriculation will equal, the intention being to keep the expenditures within the receipts."[42]

After waiting ten years, Harper was finally able to move beyond the endless discussions and proposals. Just as the university had sprung up almost overnight on the Midway ten years before, the Law School would come into being within seven months. Harper wasted no time. As Rockefeller wrote to give his blessing to the trustee's proposal, Harper made plans to meet Harvard's President Eliot in New York City and Baltimore in order to secure Eliot's counsel. The next stop was Cambridge.

Although Freund had urged Harper to single out Beale, Harper's initial approach had been to get any member of the Harvard Law School faculty as the first dean. With his characteristic boldness, he undoubtedly hoped to secure the best man. At a luncheon with the entire Harvard law faculty, he quoted the words of vision which were addressed to the Apostle Paul: "Come over into Macedonia and help us."[43]

It is not clear whether the Harvard contingent or Harper selected Beale, but Beale became the man designated to lay the Harvard foundation at Chicago. In a letter to Beale on March 14, Harper apologized for his delay in writing since their meeting in Cambridge. Eliot, reported Harper, had granted a two-year leave of absence if Beale was interested. The offer by Harper to Beale was straightforward. Beale would assume the deanship for two years. "This will require some service on your part in connection with the organization of the faculty and the announcements," Harper observed, but quickly added that "I think we can handle this without troubling you to any very great extent."[44] Harper was of the opinion that all of these assignments could be done on a single visit by Beale to Chicago for three or four days in the spring before the opening of the school on October 1.

The salary offered Beale was $5,500; Harper lamented the fact that he was unable to do more. "We should add, of course, to this, the usual deanship salary of $1,000"—thus providing Beale with one of the top salaries in legal education. Anxious to keep moving, he pushed Beale for a response by telegraph, using as a reason the hope that an announcement could be made at the next convocation. Alluding to their previous discussion, Harper indicated to Beale that no faculty commitments would be made without consultation with him. Harper had been thinking of possible faculty for some time, as he indicated in this letter: "My own opinion is that we ought to get Wigmore of the Northwestern [School of Law], and either Scott of Illinois or Mechem of Ann Arbor. I think we shall be able to secure Blewett Lee and Mr. Mack. With these as a basis, including Freund, we can proceeed further according to the demands, but in no case has there been even a consultation with any of the gentlemen named above."[45]

The response by Beale was unanticipated. Due to the sudden death of Professor James B. Thayer, Beale declined "to consider your most flattering offer." Acknowledging Harper's desire to establish "a great law school on a scholarly and liberal line," Beale was nonetheless dubious that this result could be accomplished before October 1 without sacrificing the opportunity of high standing from the start. He also felt that the new dean could not pull everything together in the three- or four-day visit to Chicago previously suggested by Harper. Beale urged Harper "to delay the establishment of your school for a year or two rather than to start without such equipment as I have indicated. I admit my lack of judgment and experience in matters of the sort, but I feel sure that it would make the difference between having a school which differs from twenty other schools in your region simply in being larger and having a school of distinction."[46]

Furthermore, Beale did not believe a school as envisioned by Harper could be opened without a library of at least 20,000 volumes. "If the faculty and students are to do scholarly work," Beale observed, "books on legal history, foreign law, and all American, English, and Canadian Reports would be needed."[47] To compile the library would require work by the dean, a librarian, and two assistant librarians. To do this within six months was viewed as impossible by Beale. Perhaps the emotions of the moment caused Beale to decline an offer he was to accept one month later. In any case his letter to Harper revealed that he had given serious thought to what was necessary, despite the initial rejection.

Despite his reservations about the library, Beale concurred with Harper on the faculty, noting that "your plan is admirable." Wigmore was described by Beale as "a man you ought to get if possible, because his scholarly tastes and his turn for writing well on legal subjects are bound, in a few years, to add distinction to any institution with which he is connected." Beale did not allude to Mechem, Freund, Lee, or Mack. He did, however, suggest that Harper consider Westengaard from Harvard and James Parker Hall from Stanford, "both of them men of high character, of attractive personality and of distinct ability as teachers."[48]

Despite his initial rejection of Harper's offer, Beale made several suggestions, based on practice at Harvard, which he hoped Harper would accept if he chose to go ahead with his plans. The faculty to be agreed upon by both men would be well-known adherents to the Harvard casebook method of teaching. In consideration of the environment of the school, Beale wondered if it might also be wise to transfer several of the Harvard students to Chicago in order to instill the spirit of Cambridge, "a spirit of industry and scholarship which is the fruit of long tradition." He suggested that a dozen men from Harvard might be induced unofficially to go to the new school for a couple of terms in order "to start with the right spirit and get tradition established there. Our students' law clubs are an important feature of our school which might be introduced bodily into yours and I had hoped that some of them might carry the methods used in editing our Law Review and that it might be possible to establish a similar publication at Chicago."[49]

By the end of March Beale had reconsidered the Chicago offer, following another visit to Cambridge by the persuasive Harper. "Since I saw you," Beale wrote to Harper, "we have consulted the faculty of law, and find no opposition to my going to you as proposed. The President approves. Nothing remains but for the Corporation to act upon my request for a leave of absence, which they will do on Monday."[50] Hearing this news, Harper, who was out of the city, telegraphed his secretary to instruct Freund to go immediately to Cambridge to talk with Beale.[51] Upon returning to Chicago, Harper wrote Freund in Cambridge in order to convey what he wished to be discussed. The assignment included three items: the preparation of a rough sketch for a law building; the best method for getting the books for the library and Beale's suggestions concerning a librarian; and Beale's reactions to the circular announcing the new Law School. Freund did not receive the letter until he returned to Chicago.[52]

The Circular of Information on the Law School had been prepared by Freund, working with Henry Pratt Judson and Harper, at the president's request in January. Because of the response the circular was to have from Harvard, it is necessary to examine several features. Listed as officers of instruction were Joseph H. Beale, Jr. (Dean), Floyd R. Mechem, Ernst Freund, Blewett Lee, and Julian W. Mack. Conforming to other university circulars, Freund prepared an introductory statement which included statements on the "Purpose" and "Distinctive Features" of the new school. Freund expressed the purpose briefly:

> The purpose of the School of Law will be: (1) to afford adequate preparation for the practice of law as a profession in any jurisdiction in which the common law prevails; and (2) to cultivate and encourage the scientific study of systematic and comparative jurisprudence, legal history, and principles of legislation.[53]

Several distinctive features were set forth by Freund. First, that the standards of admission would be such "so as to constitute the school practically a graduate school, a standard equal to that of the best schools of the country and higher than that of any school in the West." The intent was obvious: the school would be elitist, consistent with Harper's notion of graduate study, comprised of students "who have received the training which American experience and traditions have marked out as best calculated to develop intellectual power." Students would be able to save one year by coming to the school after completing three years of college work. They would then receive the bachelor's degree at the end of their first year in law school. The university would provide a prelegal curriculum in the first year of the senior college (corresponding to the third college year at other institutions), "in order that the academic training may be of the highest possible value as a preparation for the professional study of the law."[54]

The circular noted other features of the new school. The faculty would be composed of experienced law teachers, "a majority of whom have made the study of law their lifework." The opportunity for close contact between faculty and students was emphasized, as faculty would endeavor to be accessible constantly to students. Students would be expected to give full-time to the study of law; work in law offices would be discouraged. The curriculum would make special provision

for instruction in the drafting of documents and in court practice, to replace the office experience claimed by advocates of
the apprenticeship system. Law clubs would be organized for
the argument and decision of questions of law. Freund proudly
announced the plans for the library, which would have a collection of about 10,000 volumes, "an equipment, it is believed,
superior to that of any other law school in the West":

> This library will contain all the American, English and
> Canadian reports, the different collections of selected cases,
> the statutes of the several States, digests, legal magazines,
> and periodicals, recent and standard text-books, both
> English and American, and a working library in Roman and
> civil law. The students will also have the use of the general
> library and the departmental libraries of the University, con-
> taining in the aggregate approximately 350,000 volumes.[55]

The description by Freund of the arrangement of courses
and of the curriculum deserves particular note, for it was to
elicit a sharp response from Harvard. The Law School, adopting the university's quarter system, permitted a student to go
the year around, thus shortening the length of time spent in
the program. The prelaw curriculum was "intended to direct
the college work of those who expect to devote themselves to
law & studies which without being professional are related
to jurisprudence or otherwise of especial value or interest to the
future lawyer." The professional curriculum outlined appeared
to be that of the leading law schools, particularly for the first
year: contracts, torts, property, pleading, criminal law, agency,
and persons. Yet also included was international law, to be
taught by Judson, a political scientist. Moreover the elective
courses in the second and third years included several which
were not part of the standard Harvard model: international
law, constitutional law, Roman law, jurisprudence, taxation,
public officers, administrative law, municipal corporations, and
federal practice. Freund outlined a postgraduate curriculum
available only for those who had completed a three-year professional program. Freund's interests were clearly stated: "It
is expected that post-graduate work will lie to a considerable
extent in the fields of systematic and comparative jurisprudence, legal history and principles of legislation. The post-

graduate work of the Law School will be closely affiliated with the work of the Departments of History, Political Economy, Political Science, and Sociology."[56] It was this Circular of Information Freund had in hand when he headed for Cambridge at Harper's bidding.

Beale's Initial Response
"I could be of no use in
such a school."

The Harvard response to the plans for the new law school as submitted by Freund to Dean James Barr Ames and Beale was immediate and critical. In letters dated March 31 and April 2 Ames and Beale voiced to Harper their strong concern on several points. Indeed Ames asked whether the proposed loan of Beale should be dropped. "Professor Beale and I found Professor Freund a very likable man," began Ames to Harper, "but I must confess that our interviews with him have given me serious misgivings as to the wisdom of the plan of having Mr. Beale go to Chicago, even temporarily, as Dean of your new Law School."[57] For Beale the issue appeared unequivocal. He reminded Harper that the Harvard Corporation had granted him leave conditional on the notion that "the School to be established at Chicago is to have ideals and methods similar to Harvard Law School." Alluding to the circumstances resulting from the death of Professor Thayer, Beale noted to Harper: "you will remember that we consented to the inconvenience of my leaving at this time solely that I might help you establish a school on the model of the Harvard Law School. Except for this purpose (which we believe to be for the benefit of legal education) we should not have considered your proposition."[58] "Do not understand me," Ames wrote to Harper, "as believing now that this is still your wish and purpose."[59] Thus the loan of Beale, viewed from Cambridge as conditional on the creation of a law school whose curriculum, methods of study, and quality would resemble Harvard's, seemed in danger.

The source of unhappiness was Freund and Freund's ideas. Ames commented to Harper: "Knowing your high estimate of Professor Freund, and having discovered how widely his con-

ception of your new School differs in fundamentals from our
School, I feel that before further steps are taken we ought to
clear away all possibility for any subsequent misunderstanding
and disappointment."[60] Beale was less diplomatic in expressing
his disapproval to Harper: "We should have assumed that
everybody in Chicago was of the same mind, if it had not been
for the ideas Mr. Freund expressed here." Suggesting that
there would be no room for discussion, Beale divorced himself
from the ideas and methods expounded by Freund: "He seemed
to be cognizant of your plans for a school, and what he had in
mind was absolutely opposed to our ideas and methods. I could
be of no use in such a school."[61] Both Ames and Beale proceeded to explain to Harper the differences of opinion between
the Harvard position and the opinions coming from the Midway.

First, concerning the curriculum, Freund had suggested that
two-ninths of the work offered in the Law School be courses
which Harvard viewed as belonging properly in the departments of political science or sociology. The Harvard position
was the traditional one taken by the few law schools which
had considered the issue. Subjects related to the liberal arts did
not belong in legal education, and those deemed slightly questionable were assigned to seminars. "We have no such subjects in our Curriculum," Ames noted proudly in regard to
the Freund proposal, "and are unanimously opposed to the
teaching of anything but pure law in our department." Ames
quickly added, in response to Freund's notions of postgraduate
study, "nor would the transfer of such subjects to a post-
graduate year in the School accord with our conception of the
true fashion of a law school."[62] For Beale the Freund proposal
for integrating subjects outside traditional law courses into
legal education, even in the third year, was unthinkable, for it
reduced the time available for students to study "pure" law.
"He wishes to put into the three-year course certain subjects
which are not law in any sense," Beale complained to Harper,
"and to that extent to diminish the time and thought devoted
to the study of law. This is a very serious matter, and one
which I regard as of radical importance."[63]

Citing evidence that Freund was advocating the inclusion
of legal courses different in length from the courses given in

the best schools, Beale noted that, although the length of a course was in some way arbitrarily determined, "the fact that the Schools have arrived at a tacit agreement in the matter suggests that the law is most naturally taught in that way." Beale's unhappiness was strongly expressed. Observing that Columbia had unwisely allowed students to take a handful of nonlegal electives from their School of Political Science, he denounced such a move, belittling Columbia: "these facts have been suggested as accountable for the striking failure of the school to take the position to which her location, her wealth, and the ability of her faculty seem to entitle her." Beale took a hard stand on the question of curriculum, and insisted "that no subjects shall be taught in the School or counted toward the degree but strictly legal subjects. The degree shall be given only after a three-year study of such subjects."[64]

The next point of contention concerned the faculty. Here again Freund's notions were viewed as heretical. The opinion expounded unequivocally from Cambridge was that only people teaching "pure law" could be faculty. "The faculty determines in the first instance all matters of general policy within the school," Beale observed, "and is composed solely of persons who teach *law* in the strict sense of the word." Beale resorted to the Harvard experience and traditions to support his argument: "we think that experience justifies us in believing that in this way alone we can turn out thoroughly trained men, fit at once to enter upon the practice of a learned and strenuous profession."

Ames also maintained that Freund's recommendation to admit to the law faculty professors who taught political science and sociology was incorrect. "We think that no one but a lawyer, teaching law, should be a member of a Law Faculty." Consequently the second demand upon Harper by his newly appointed dean was that "the policy of the School shall be formulated in the first instance by a faculty consisting only of lawyers. Of course I do not mean that the faculty shall be independent of trustees of other governing bodies, but that it shall not be filled with men who are not lawyers, and have had no experience as teachers in a law school." Furthermore, Beale asked for one more assurance from Harper that "no person shall teach in the school who does not frankly concur in adopting for the school the spirit and the methods of the Harvard Law School."[65]

The problem of faculty spirit and solidarity was crucial to Beale, who wanted no nonlawyer on the faculty. Without the complete sympathy of the faculty he could not accomplish what he had been asked to do. For Beale, the notion of unanimous commitment to the ideals and aims of the school was the factor responsible for the creation of an exceptional institution. "Where so many good law schools exist, a school can stand at the head only by doing as well as possible everything it has to do." Continuing his argument for consensus by the faculty, Beale again warned Harper he would not come to Chicago without unqualified support: "if the plan of the school is to be such as I approve, all the other teachers should approve it; if not, I must not be there to create discord."[66]

There were other points of unhappiness expressed by Dean Ames in his exchange with Harper. Although Ames did not "pretend to know" which department within the university should handle prelaw instruction, he was firmly persuaded that "it would be altogether foreign to our ideas to have it in the Law School. We believe the success of our School is due in no small degree to the solidarity of our Faculty and to its concentration upon the work of teaching the law pure and simple." Ames also indicated concern that there would be no building available for the exclusive use of the Law School until January 1903.

But perhaps the greatest problem for Ames involved the method of study. The Harvard method was the case method and had been established only after Langdell and Ames had fought for it in a major battle within the Harvard faculty. "Our School," Ames told Harper, "is conspicuous for its belief in the learning of law by the systematic study of Cases. If Professor Beale is to be Dean with the purpose of reproducing the Harvard method, he must have a faculty that believes in that method."[67] Ames conceded that he had not asked Freund for his view on that issue. Yet his fear was indicated. "Certainly his [Freund's] belief in the general methods of the German Universities, and his general views as to the function of a law school would predispose him against a thoroughgoing belief in us or our methods."[68] The issue was basic for Ames, and he questioned the appointment of Mechem on the grounds that it was uncertain whether Mechem believed in the case method: "Professor Mechem as a law teacher, is also, to me, an unknown quantity." Ames could not see any possibility for Beale's success until "he is assured that he is to have a body of colleagues who will support him loyally because of their belief in him and his methods."[69]

Harper had conveyed earlier to Ames and Beale the hesitancy of the trustees and certain members of the Chicago bar in accepting completely the Harvard model. The various positions on legal education expressed to Harper had filtered out to Cambridge, culminating with Freund's visit. After summarizing the major points of difference, Ames threw the problem back to Harper, allowing him the opportunity to withdraw gracefully from the arrangement: "Bearing in mind your statements that Chicago lawyers regard our methods with distrust, and that the lawyers on your Board of Trustees, in particular, do not believe in us and knowing your high estimate of the probable influence and effectiveness of Professor Freund in the proposed Law Faculty, I can readily understand that, whatever may be your personal inclinations, you may, upon reflection, deem it inexpedient to invite Professor Beale to come to you upon these terms."[70]

Beale too voiced his unhappiness with the situation. Harper simply had to choose between Harvard and Freund. Unless the faculty shared with him complete sympathy for his ideas, Beale would not come. "These differences of view are so fundamental that it is obviously necessary to choose one conception of the school or the other," Beale asserted. "I cannot spare the time to go from here and teach a short time in a school which I do not believe to be wisely organized; nor if I am to introduce Harvard methods in parts of two years, with the bench and the trustees lukewarm, can I accomplish anything unless the faculty is in hearty sympathy with the plan." Thus the final demand made by Beale to Harper was linked to the initial premise of the contract: "that you yourself will heartily support me in the effort to establish in your new school 'ideals and methods similar to those of the Harvard Law School.' "[71]

The issues were sharply drawn and the demands clearly expressed. Beale's final request forced the next move on Harper. "As soon as I get your answer, if you wish still to have me at the head of the only kind of school I could teach in, I shall be able to go on to Chicago, meet the other members of the faculty, and discuss details of the organization."[72] Ames concluded his letter cautiously by allowing that the Harvard Corporation would be content should Harper choose not to invite Beale as dean of the Law School. "Nor shall we lose our interest in your School," Ames prophetically concluded. "On the contrary we shall watch its development under favorable auspices, upon lines different from ours, with the hope that it may not only achieve a distinct success, but that it may throw new light upon the problem of legal education."[73]

Thus an impasse arose as Ames and Beale responded to the plans for the new school as outlined by Freund and demanded that Harper give "distinct and definite assurances" that their requests be met. After waiting nearly ten years for the right moment to proceed with his plans for a law school, Harper was faced with an unanticipated situation. He had sought carefully ideas and support from within the university, the trustees, the bar, and the community. His vision of the second influential wing called for by Judge Kohlsaat which would be integral to the purpose of the university had suddenly met with opposition. But the impasse would be momentary and the controversy would quietly disappear.

4   Building a Faculty

Beale backed down for reasons not entirely clear, perhaps because he wanted the job. There is no indication that Harper gave either written or verbal assurances to the demands from Ames and Beale. And the strongly stated positions set forth from Harvard were not repeated. The events that happened in the next several months demonstrated that the largest part of the Harvard-Chicago controversy was resolved in favor of Cambridge, although significant departures from the Harvard model were to occur and would have a major impact on American legal education. Once Beale agreed to come, the immediate task was to identify and recruit faculty—a major project, given the time-limit of six months before the first classes were to begin. If Harper was to see his dream of a major law school materialize, the quality of the initial faculty was of first concern, for these people would establish the reputation of the Law School. With the urgent and numerous responsibilities involved in organizing the school, the tension between conflicting theories of legal education cooled.

Beale Comes to Chicago
and the Organization Begins

Writing to Freund on April 7, 1902, after accepting Harper's offer, Beale stepped back from his unequivocal position as expressed to Harper and noted that "Ames was more disturbed than I by what he (and I) consider your heretical views about the law. The hard fight which he and Mr. Langdell had in this faculty years ago made him anxious that I would not meet a similar difficulty." Beale's cheerful accommodation was in sharp contrast to his previously expressed intransigence; as the controversy subsided, he appeared eager to reduce any friction between himself and his new colleague. Gracefully Beale transferred to Mechem the brunt of responsibility for stimulating Ames's sharp response. Ames's major concern, according to Beale, was that "Professor Mechem might come spoiling for a fight as to policy."[1]

As to his own position, Beale told Freund that he was concerned about Chicago's questioning of the case method and the injection of political science courses into "pure law." Beale feared the influence of political science faculty in the Law School: "the faculty might be made up largely of political science men. . . . The very eminence of Professor Judson and the others would give their ideas over-powering weight."[2] The assurances initially demanded from Harper by Beale were never explicitly made. All of the Harvard positions would be modified, as the plans for Harper's Law School came into being. The clash subsided quickly once Beale arrived at Chicago and the organizational work began in the spring of 1902 under Beale's spirited leadership. This indicates that perhaps Beale agreed to come because of the challenges involved with establishing a new law school which might rival his own.

Beale and Freund developed a strong working relationship (it was, after all, Freund who had initially suggested to Harper that Beale was the right man to direct the creation of the law school). At Freund's last convocation in Chicago, he introduced Beale and warmly stressed his contributions. Despite the fact Beale had been a part-time dean, Freund suggested that his influence had been central to the preliminary stages of the school's history:

> I am sure that all who are connected with the Law School are agreed that experience has demonstrated the wisdom of even this arrangement—an arrangement which illustrated in a striking manner the spirit of goodwill and co-operation between the great institution of the East and her younger rival in the West.
>
> This is not the time or place to speak of results or prospects; but I may be permitted to give expression to the gratitude which we feel for the help he has given us, and to the gratification which has come from co-operating,

though for all too brief a period, with one whose freshness
and vigor of mind, and whose love of sound law, has been
a constant stimulus and inspiration to his colleagues and
his students.[3]

Both the Harvard views and Freund's influence would be
deeply felt in the first chapter of Chicago's history. Although
Freund and Beale gave endless hours to the organization of the
school, there is some evidence that Beale was never completely
enamored of this man upon whom Harper had strongly relied
and who was to be a major figure in initiating changes in the
standard law school curriculum. In a report of progress to
President Eliot on November 5, 1903, Beale makes no reference
to Freund, although he speaks of the other faculty quite
generously:

> Hall I find not only a successful teacher, but a delightful
> man to work with, and one on whose advice I rely. Whittier,
> I regret to say, has been ill ever since the opening of the
> school . . . the students are almost as high quality as at
> Harvard; and both the teachers from Northwestern and
> Stanford and the students who have come to us from other
> schools speak of the difference in the quality of instruction
> and the severity of the work. Mack, Hall and I heartily
> agree that the system we adopted with hesitation, that of
> spending all the time upon three subjects . . . is a thoroughly
> desirable one.[4]

Although certain courses promoted by Freund, like railroad
transportation and relation of state to industry, were not included in the curriculum, a course called "Elements in International Law," taught by Judson, was offered as an elective,
and, of course, Freund's innovative instruction in administrative law was introduced. There is further evidence of give-and-
take between Freund and Beale in the fact that constitutional
law was not to be taught by Judson, as proposed by Freund,
but by Freund and James Parker Hall, a protégé of Beale's.
Judson was to teach federal constitutional law.

In the merger of the technical insight of Beale with the innovative ideas of Freund, a blend of the traditional and the new
took place and resulted in the first significant effort to liberalize
the curriculum of legal education since the Langdell efforts at

Harvard. Edward Levi suggests that Freund and Beale both began with the fundamental principle of establishing excellence in the core program of the law curriculum. Both men wanted legal education to reflect an appropriate response to the changing needs within society. If they disagreed over the means, they at least shared the concern that legal education should confront squarely the question of how the emerging disciplines in academia related to the study of law:

> These great men—and each of them was great—were concerned that the law curriculum establish excellence in the core program. They were concerned also as to the feasibility of expanding the program to meet the growing demands on lawyers—hence, the reference to accounting or government regulation of business. They were in dispute as to how to make sure that legal education kept abreast of the developments of the newer disciplines and how to provide that the lawyer, in addition to his general education and his specifically legal training, would have special contact with the application of the newer disciplines to public affairs.[5]

The First Faculty

On April 12, five days after Beale had written his conciliatory letter to Freund, Harper informed the University Senate that Beale had consented to come. Time was running short; the opening of the Law School was less than six months away. Beale had agreed to the hiring of several faculty members in a previous exchange with Harper, who then proceeded to steal Julian W. Mack and Blewett Lee from Northwestern. Harper had also arranged for Freund to be transferred from the Department of Political Science to the law faculty. He then moved ahead in an attempt to get Floyd R. Mechem from Michigan and James Parker Hall and Clarke Butler Whittier from Stanford. With unrelenting persistence, Harper acted quickly to draw together what would become the strongest law faculty in the United States.

The raid on the Northwestern faculty yielded two of the strongest law teachers in America and left Northwestern floundering; Mack and Dean John Henry Wigmore had been the only two resident faculty members remaining. There had been discussion earlier of also securing Wigmore. Harper appeared anxious initially to get him, perhaps because of Beale's strong recommendation. But Harper's efforts were unsuccessful. The Northwestern trustees waged a successful effort to persuade Wigmore of his moral obligations to Northwestern. On April 9, 1902, Harper wired Beale in Boston: "Wigmore wavering under great pressure brought to bear by Northwestern. Could you write him?"[6]

But Wigmore would not be moved. Harper became bitter over this episode. The next year Beale pushed Harper to appoint Wigmore as dean and tried to eliminate the misunderstanding which had risen. Conceding to Harper that Wigmore had used bad judgment in regard to the negotiations, Beale noted that Columbia was also trying to persuade Wigmore to leave Northwestern: "I know that a misunderstanding has grown up between you; but knowing Wigmore as I do I feel sure that while he may be lacking in judgment he *cannot* have been intellectually dishonest. Under those circumstances, considering the obvious advantages in many ways of having him with us, I hope you would approve of trying to get him for us."[7] But Harper would not budge and squelched further discussion. Responding to Beale, Harper stated: "I cannot persuade myself that Wigmore has the ideals which we wish to characterize our Law School. His own statements made to me clearly convince me of this fact; besides, I am very sure that his spirit is not the spirit which we would like to have developed in our work." "I speak of this," Harper added, "entirely outside of the question of dishonesty to which you refer."[8]

The appointment of Julian Mack brought together two Cambridge friends, and Beale must have been delighted that his classmate and close friend would assist in establishing the new venture. Mack was born in San Francisco but grew up in Cincinnati.[9] Although he did not attend college, Mack was accepted into the Harvard Law School as a member of the class of 1887. He was chosen class orator and received his LL.B. cum laude. With Beale he had been a founder of the *Harvard Law Review* and a member of its first board of editors. Following law school, he was awarded the first Parker Scholarship by Harvard, an award that enabled him to study civil law and legal philosophy for three years (1887–90) at the universities of Berlin and Leipzig. Thus, like Freund, he was exposed to and influenced by the German system of legal education. He was admitted to the bar of the supreme courts and of the federal courts of Ohio and Illinois in 1890 and began an active practice. In 1895 he became a professor of law at Northwestern.

Blewett Lee had also combined a career of practice and teaching prior to his appointment at Chicago. Born in 1867 in Columbus, Mississippi, the son of one of the surviving commanders of the Confederate Army, Lee was graduated from the Agricultural and Mechanical College of Mississippi with a B.S. in 1883. He then spent two years in study at the University of Virginia and afterward attended Harvard, where he was graduated in 1888 with the degrees of LL.B. and A.M. Then he went to Europe and, like Mack and others in the Chicago group, became acquainted with the German universities, studying for a year in Leipzig and Freiberg. Upon his return to America he served as secretary to Justice Gray of the U.S. Supreme Court. For three years he practiced law in Atlanta, a period during which he became a member of the first faculty of the Atlanta Law School. He then came to Chicago, accepting an offer to join the faculty at Northwestern where he taught carriers, corporations, and constitutional law. He continued to have an active practice and resigned his teaching responsibilities in 1902 to become general attorney for the Illinois Central Railroad Company. In 1897 Harvard made a strong bid to get Lee to return to his alma mater, an episode that caused some embarrassment for Harvard. In rejecting the offer, Lee noted that Northwestern permitted him to maintain full-time practice while teaching and that accepting the Harvard offer "would involve some pecuniary sacrifice and giving up of the practice of my profession to which I am considerably attached." Apparently the newspapers learned of Lee's rejection, for several days later Lee wrote an apologetic letter to Eliot over the publicity, claiming that a friend had read the offer from Dean Ames and indiscreetly talked.[10]

Harper Tries for Mechem

Prior to the first faculty meeting on April 17, Harper had already begun his attempt to entice Floyd R. Mechem from Michigan. Despite the uncertainty expressed by Ames about

Mechem's ability, Harper chose to follow the counsel of Freund, Galusha Anderson, and others who urged Mechem's appointment. On March 24 Harper, hoping to gain Mechem's advice on the new law school, wrote to him asking whether he planned to be in Chicago in the near future. "Although we have never met," Harper wrote, "I do not feel that we are utter strangers, in view of the many appreciative words which our boys have given me concerning your work with them."[11] Mechem had been at Michigan since 1891 and held the Tappan Professorship in Law there. Born in New York in 1858, Mechem grew up in Michigan and attended high school in Ann Arbor.[12] Unable to attend college or law school due to financial reasons, he taught school part-time and devoted his evenings to the reading of law. In 1879 he was admitted to the bar at Marshall, Michigan, and began the practice of law in Battle Creek with the man who had directed his law studies, a Mr. Wadleigh. For eight years he practiced law and for four terms served as city attorney.

In 1887 he moved to Detroit, where he established the firm of Mechem and Beaumont. Responding to the need for an adequate book for the practitioner on the subject of agency, Mechem published in 1889 *A Treatise on the Law of Agency.* A laudatory review in the *Harvard Law Review* noted that Mechem had carefully classified the different branches of "the law under discussion, and divided and subdivided its topics in a most admirable manner; in fact, one is almost led to believe that the law can be reduced to an exact science after reading Mr. Mechem's simple though exhaustive classification of the law of agency."[13] Encouraged by this reception, Mechem went on to write a number of scholarly works: *A Treatise on the Law of Public Offices and Officers* (1890), the only treatise, English or American, on this subject; a revision of *Hutchins on Carriers* (1891); *The Law of Agency* (1893); *The Law of Damages* (1893); *The Law of Succession* (1895); and *The Law of Partnerships* (1896).

Mechem's interest in legal education went beyond the efforts mentioned above and numerous articles in magazines and journals. While practicing in Detroit he was instrumental in the organization of the Detroit College of Law. Concerned with the practical implications of legal education, Mechem was in charge of the Practice Court at the University of Michigan. He felt strongly that the law faculty should be involved in the restatement of the law:

> With the enormous growth in bulk of our law, with the increasing output of reports, with the constantly increasing number of new questions caused by the wonderful changes in our social and economic conditions, there is a constant and increasing demand that some persons shall sift and analyze and restate the principles of law which are being applied. Nowhere else can this be so intelligently and thoroughly done as by the law teachers of the country. Into the law schools, as into great laboratories, all these new ideas in law schools should come to be tested, compared, analyzed and reported upon.[14]

It is understandable how Harper would be drawn to a man intent on viewing legal education as a process of discovery and one who viewed the law school as a laboratory.

Mechem also believed the law school to be an appropriate place for the pursuit of research. "The Law Schools of this country," Mechem insisted, "must be places wherein the most original and most scholarly legal investigation is carried on. The law teacher has, upon the whole, the best opportunity for this work." The practicing lawyer could not find time to move beyond the mastery of a particular subject without the availability of outstanding library facilities. The law professor, suggested Mechem, has the "advantage of consultation with his colleagues who are also experts in cognate fields and he has the opportunity of hearing the discussions and answering the objections of successive classes of bright students whose arguments in many cases, as those who hear me will bear witness, would do credit to the older members of the Bar."[15]

In regard to his opinions on the proper method of teaching, Mechem was an "unknown quantity" from the Harvard point of view. Despite the fact that he wrote casebooks, Mechem did not give unqualified support to the case method: "I think we are inclined in these days to say too much about methods and to convey the impression that some of us think we have a sort of patent upon the only right way, and that if the student will only pursue our method he will have a guaranty of success." Mechem said that perhaps for the ends sought the study of cases was the best method. Yet the qualification was ever present: "Professor Dwight was a great teacher under one method, Professor Langdell under another and Judge Cooley under still another." To be a good law professor, Mechem suggested, one had to have experience. Although he viewed teaching as a full-time profession, he did not subscribe to the opinion held by Ames and others that one could teach without practical experience. "Law is so distinctively a practical science," Mechem observed, "it exists so necessarily for practical ends, so many elements enter into its operation and effect beside pure theory or clear logic, that some experience with the practical seems to me to be essential."[16]

At Michigan Mechem taught the science of jurisprudence, damages, taxation, partnership, and the administration and distribution of the estates of deceased persons. He supported the attempts at Michigan by President James B. Angell to develop a sense of intellectual unity among departments, particularly in the joint efforts involving the literary and professional departments. He also created a course in higher commercial education, which was described as an effort "to adjust instruction to the needs of practical life without destroying the culture and scholarship which a university education ought to bestow."[17] He was concerned about the absence of legal history in the curriculum. "Nowhere else is there likely to be found either the temper, the time, or the facilities for this important work." Central to legal education was the study of jurisprudence. "Nothing in my judgment," maintained Mechem, "can be of greater interest and importance than the careful study into the nature of the law, the analysis of legal ideas and the correlation and comparison of legal rules."[18]

His advice to his students revealed Mechem's insistence that students analyze and classify their work in order to see the relation of each subject to the other. He urged them to go beyond the mere language of the law in question, to the reason of the law: "to so associate each principle with some leading case in which it was applied that the principle itself shall be to him not a mere abstraction but a living force operating upon actual facts in such wise as to at once suggest the manner and the limit of its application."[19]

Harper had to wait only a week for a careful response from
Mechem, who stated three conditions necessary for his re-
moval from Michigan. The first concerned Mechem's desire to
be in charge of all subjects concerning public law, in particular
constitutional law, taxation, and the law of public officers and
offices. He also noted his decade-long interest in the science of
jurisprudence. Second, Mechem hoped that his work would be
arranged so as to allow "a reasonable amount of leisure for research and writing" as well as the liberty to "keep in touch
with the practical side of the profession by a limited amount of
consultation practice, if the opportunity should present itself."
He believed, said Mechem, "that this is one way, much
neglected, in which the University expert may make himself
useful and extend the influence of the university." Third, "I
should expect that my salary shall be of the highest class paid
to professors in the School of Law. I am not mercenary, but I
am jealous of that sort of professional standing which comparative salaries usually indicate." Mechem continued by indicating satisfaction with his current position combined with
a curious desire in regard to the plans underway at Chicago:

> I realize, however, that the establishment of your new Law
> School presents an opportunity, which I feel assured will
> be improved to the uttermost—of gathering together a
> group of first class men, and of founding a school of Law
> upon such lines that connection with it may be a credit,
> and the opportunity to assist in creating it may be a
> pleasure. It is this possibility which appeals to me, and I
> therefore am led to say, as I said at the outset, that if you
> are still of mind to make me a proposal, and can see your
> way clear to make it upon the conditions I have indicated,
> I shall be ready to consider it.[20]

Harper's response was immediate. In regard to Mechem's
first condition Harper noted that there was only one person,
Freund, whose work overlapped with Mechem's in the area of
law of public officers and offices. Harper quickly added that
Freund's desire to continue this work would be satisfied if he
could offer a course occasionally during a summer quarter.
Harper also said that Freund consented to allow Mechem to
be in charge of the subjects listed by Mechem but cautioned

him that the science of jurisprudence might be offered only as an elective. As to Mechem's request for time for research and consultation, Harper responded by emphasizing the necessity of an organic relationship between the Law School and the university, a relationship that would satisfy Mechem's concern:

> Great emphasis will be placed upon the fact that the University spirit is to prevail in the work of the Law School, and it is desired that every man in the faculty shall have a large amount of leisure for research and writing. There is every reason further, why it would be to the advantage of the University, as well as to yourself, to have you keep in touch with the practical side of the profession by a limited amount of consultation practice.[21]

The third request was easy for Harper, for he knew that no American law schools were paying salaries higher than the $5,500 he was offering. "In case a higher salary is at any time paid to the professors of the School of Law, and I have no doubt that this will be done soon," Harper shrewdly noted, "your salary would be increased to the highest point."[22]

This time Mechem was slower in responding. When he did write, he said that Harper's letter answered his requests "fully, frankly and satisfactorily." Citing the fact that he and Mrs. Mechem had wanted to check the living conditions on the Midway, Mechem said that the authorities at Michigan had asked him to reserve his final decision until after the Board of Regents met. "There are also," he noted "certain moral obligations of the sort of which I spoke to you, being urged against my going." Yet Mechem's conclusions were positive to the point that he offered to meet with the Chicago faculty in their preliminary discussions. "I must say, however, that I expect to come."[23]

Harper weighed carefully his response and drew up two telegrams, both dated the same day, to send to Mechem. The first telegram is edited in pencil and probably was not sent: "We think Michigan Regents have exaggerated obligation. We feel you ought not yield because of these representations. Such representations are frequently made in similar cases without basis. While no legal obligation to us, is there not also moral obligation toward Chicago?" The last sentence was crossed out in pencil. The other telegram directly put pressure on Mechem to consider his moral obligations to Chicago. "May I suggest," Harper said, "that you must have concluded previous to your last visit that your moral obligations toward Michigan did not prevent acceptance of our offer. Should you allow your own judgment to be determined by others now that you have assumed some obligation toward us by joining in our preliminary work?"[24] Yet despite the fact that Mechem had by then participated in the preliminary discussions, he had made up his mind to stay at Michigan for one more year.

Responding to Harper upon receipt of the telegram, Mechem apologized profusely for the situation and any possible embarrassment to Chicago. "I realize that in order to satisfy moral obligations here, I am disappointing expectations there," Mechem lamented, "and I regret more than I can tell you that I have permitted myself to get into this predicament." The major reason, Mechem suggested, was that Professor Wilgus was leaving. Mechem went on to say that Harper would undoubtedly learn that Michigan's regents had proposed to increase his salary and reduce his work, yet he hastened to add that this had not influenced his decision, "especially as it is still financially to my disadvantage."[25]

Writing a letter the same afternoon to Mechem, Harper could not conceal his disappointment as he doggedly pursued the outside chance: "Could you not arrange to come in the middle of the year? We want you and we want you very much. We are ready to do anything that is possible to have you carry out the original plan."[26] Mechem's reply was optimistic, for he noted that he had agreed to stay only another year. "It seems to me that by the expiration of that period I should have satisfied every form of moral obligation that I may be under by reason of my undertakings here."[27] Ultimately the exciting prospects of the new law school on the Midway and Harper's persistence were to win out, but the first year would not include Mechem, described by Beale as "the best-known teacher of law in the West, easily the foremost teacher at the largest law school in the country, and probably the foremost legal authority now writing in the country."[28]

Harper and Ames Compete
for James Parker Hall

The disappointed Harper shared the Mechem correspondence
with Beale, who had returned to Cambridge. Asking Beale
where to turn next, Harper said: "I can understand his embarrassment, but I thought he was thoroughly committed to
us."[29] The same letter, however, contained good news, for
Harper told Beale of the acceptance of James Parker Hall. Born
in Frewsburg, New York in 1873, Hall attended high school in
Jamestown, New York. He was an exceptional student at
Cornell University, receiving a Phi Beta Kappa key in his
junior year and serving as one of the Woodward orators as
well as commencement orator in his senior year. Graduating
from Cornell, where he expressed interest in engineering, in
1894 he nonetheless attended Harvard Law School, graduating
cum laude in 1897. During his stay at Cambridge he was president of the Harvard Union. In 1897 he was admitted to the
New York bar and practiced with the Buffalo firm of Bissell,
Carey and Cooke. In 1898–1900 Hall lectured on real property
and constitutional law at the Buffalo Law School. He then went
to Stanford in 1900 to accept the appointment of associate professor, abandoning the active practice of law. Hall's was the
first name suggested by Beale in his preliminary discussion
with Harper.

With his customary directness, Harper pursued Hall vigorously, aware of the fact that Harvard and then Columbia were
trying to get him. In a telegram on April 11, Harper queried:
"Would you consider proposition to accept professorship in
school of law just being established in University of Chicago?
If so, on what conditions?" Harper then followed this up with
a letter in which he mentioned that Mechem would be coming,
as well as Mack and Lee. Suggesting that a new building would
be erected for $200,000 and that $50,000 would be allocated
for books, Harper offered Hall a full professorship. "We are
hoping that you may see your way clear to join us in Chicago,"
Harper continued, "and help establish a new school which
shall have the spirit and methods of the Harvard School and
do for the west what Harvard has done for the east. The faculty is a most excellent one as thus far constituted. We spent

last evening working over details, and the spirit of co-opera-
tion was of the heartiest character."[30]

Hall was clearly interested. In a telegram dated April 19,
he told Harper that he expected to accept the offer but wanted
more particulars.[31] Harper responded: "Beale of Harvard
Dean. Methods and spirit like Harvard. Beale suggests you
take Commercial Law and Evidence or Equity. Full professorship salary fifty-five hundred dollars. We know Harvard offer.
Have written other colleagues Mechem of Michigan probably
Mack and Lee with them."[32] Harper did know about Harvard's
offer, which proposed an assistant professorship with a salary
of $2,500 "and promotion in two years if successful."[33] Hall's
letter of acceptance to Harper was written on April 21. The delay is accounted for by Hall, who told Harper pointedly that he
had waited for a response from Harvard's Ames, "whom I
asked for advice upon your offer independently of their own
proposition. Both came yesterday and both were so satisfactory that I had no further hesitation."[34] A telegram from Hall
to Eliot on April 15 suggested that Hall's initial inclination was
toward his alma mater. He had queried Eliot: "Chicago offers
full professorship at $5,500. Can you give $4,000 and let me
teach constitutional law as one of my courses?"[35] Undoubtedly
Hall was attracted by the salary at Chicago, for he noted to
Harper that he was grateful for the offer, "which to a man of
my age seems particularly generous and attractive." Moreover
Hall was drawn to the excitement of being involved in the organization of a new law school. "When I came here two years
ago," Hall noted in regard to Stanford, "our school was
then for the first time organized on a three year basis and
it has been a great pleasure helping to put it in good running order. The same kind of work at Chicago ought to be
still more enjoyable under your much more favorable
conditions."[36]

Harper's reputation for stealing distinguished professors by
means of seductive offers was well established in educational
circles. Dean Ames tried to console President Eliot over his loss
by saying that Hall probably "found that he could not honor-
ably withdraw his invitation to [the University of] Chicago."[37]
Stanford's president, David Starr Jordan, wrote a friendly
letter to Harper concerning Hall:

In taking our Professor Hall you have made a great
break in our flourishing young Law School. I congratulate
you on having secured him. I think there is no more promising young man to be found on the list of professors in
any institution in the country. His ultimate strength will
lie in his power of investigation and his marked cleverness
of intellect. I am glad to see him receive the promotion he
deserves, even though we were not quite able to give it
here.[38]

Harper's reply expressed appreciation to Jordan for the courtesy of his letter. "I am sure that Hall is a strong man, and I
am sure that you are making a great contribution to the new
law school of the University of Chicago in permitting him to
come to us."[39]

Beale expressed delight to Harper that his favorite candidate
had accepted. Possibly to heal the wounds over Harper's lost
battle for Wigmore, Beale prophesied that ultimately Hall
would prove to be the greater man: "There is no doubt in my
mind that within a few years he [Hall] will stand head and
shoulders above Wigmore as a legal scholar and I believe will
be quite as good as a teacher." Beale continued by suggesting
reasons why Hall chose Chicago over Harvard: "The dignity
of a full professorship and the better choice of subjects, I
think, influenced him."[40]

This was not to be the last time that Harvard would try to
get Hall and be confronted with the issue of salaries and the
other attractions of Harper's law school. The next summer
Eliot made another unsuccessful attempt, much to the chagrin
of Dean Ames, who knew his salaries were not competitive.
Writing to Eliot, Ames noted that Williston and Beale were
receiving $4,500 and that Hall had been offered $5,000. He
then continued to prod Eliot on the question of salaries, urging
him to consider the law faculty apart from other departments.
He expressed concern over the Chicago salaries. "Wyman can
go to Chicago at any time. . . . Williston has been offered
$7,000 to go to Columbia."[41] Harvard's attempt to get Hall
from Chicago is an interesting undercurrent to the outwardly
friendly relationship between the institutions. Unquestionably, Ames was unhappy with his own faculty situation;

within a year after Harper's law school was established he expressed great concern over the "formidable" rival.[42] Thus Ames complained to Eliot: "I cannot share your sanguine view as to the attractive power of Harvard if they [Chicago] remain as they are. I think too our faculty must strengthen quickly. Gray, as you have said, is not successful with the important courses of Evidence and Constitutional Law. Smith, while excellent in Torts, leaves much to desire in working with the third year course in Corporation. Wambaugh and Brannan are moderately successful. Strobel is a cipher as far as the Law School is concerned."[43]

In order to recruit the distinguished faculty which he enticed to the Midway, Harper paid handsomely. He knew it and Eliot knew it. Harper's argument to the trustees soon after the school opened, on the issue of law faculty salaries, is revealing. First he argued that top salaries were necessary as it was extremely difficult to find strong men willing to give themselves to teaching law. He also noted that Columbia and Harvard had been actively recruiting three of the faculty. Further, Harper stressed the "importance from the point of view of maintaining the work of the Law School on its present basis of creating a confidence in the faculty itself that its best members may not be tempted to join Columbia and Harvard Schools at their suggestion." Thus at Chicago a professor received $5,500 when appointed, $6,000 after five years, $6,750 after another five years, and $7,500 after the next five years. The top salary was $8,000.[44]

The comparable salaries at Harvard were $4,000, $4,500, $5,000, and $5,500.[45] Ames also noted the provisions at Chicago for a retirement allowance, which Harvard did not provide. In order for Harvard to do some raiding to improve the quality of its faculty, Ames suggested:

> If we were to have a scale of salaries $500 less than that of Chicago, I believe we could tempt away any of their good men who could come on any terms. If the difference was greater than that we must be prepared to see Chicago building a formidable rival of our Faculty. . . . Just as soon as our younger men begin to feel that our School with its ample funds treats them in a parsimonious spirit it will be

difficult not only to bring to us new men from other
Schools paying larger salaries, but also to keep them
here.[46]

Ames tried to understand Eliot's reluctance to give salary
preference to law faculty in relation to other Harvard faculty
but refused to accept Eliot's position. "I am not, as you suggest,
discouraged, but apprehensive lest a raison [sic] for uniformity
may injure the Law School. I see no reason why," Ames insisted, "a department which has a surplus should fail to pay
adequate salaries, because other departments with no surplus
or with a deficit cannot do the same thing."[47] The failure to get
Hall was a severe disappointment to Eliot and Ames and a major victory for Harper, who would eventually name Hall to
succeed Beale as dean, a position Hall would then hold for
twenty-four years.

The Recruitment of Whittier
The Faculty Begins Its Work

Harper sent Hall the official acknowledgment of his acceptance, and asked him to exert influence on Clarke Butler Whittier, the final professor asked to serve on the first faculty.[48]
Whittier, who was born in St. Louis in 1872, grew up in
Toronto, Canada, and later in southern California, where he
graduated in the first class of Riverside High School. He spent
two years at the University of the Pacific until Stanford University began classes in 1891. Majoring in history, he received
his A.B. in 1893. For two years he studied at Harvard Law
School and then took a leave of absence for a year to practice
in Los Angeles. In 1896 he received his LL.B. from Harvard.
Following a decision to make the teaching of law his permanent career, he studied history and economics at Stanford for
one year and during that time was invited to join the law
faculty there. Like Hall, he had worked with Dean Nathan
Abbott in organizing the Stanford Law School.

Harper had little trouble in recruiting Whittier and apparently turned to him largely because of Beale's advice, who a
year later was to propose to Harper that Whittier might be a
good acting dean.[49] His offer, as noted in a telegram of April
28, was mild in contrast to the other offers: "Would you con-

sider proposition of professorship in new faculty of law. Salary fifty-five hundred. Answer. Beale very anxious."[50] The response was positive. The initial faculty was complete. Although other names had been discussed, Beale informed Harper that another full-time professor would not be desirable and that "it will hardly be necessary now to consider any other names."[51] On May 1 the trustees approved the faculty, noting that Mack would work only five-eighths of the time and Lee one-quarter of the time. It is interesting that the only faculty member whose base pay was not approved at $5,500 was Ernst Freund, who received $1,000 for extra services rendered during the year and a salary of $3,500 from October 1, 1902.[52] Two days later Harper announced to the University Council that the "Law Faculty had been completed with six members, Professor Beale of the Harvard Law School as Dean." Harper could certainly be proud of the quality of the faculty recruited in less than three months, a faculty later to be considered—after the addition of Mechem and Harry A. Bigelow—as probably the greatest law faculty in American legal education.

In the meantime much work needed to be done by the new faculty, who were invited by Harper to meet at the Chicago Club on April 17, coinciding with Beale's visit to Chicago. The first item of business was approval of the motion calling for Chicago to join the recently established American Association of Law Schools. Beale was designated the official representative to attend the summer meetings in Saratoga. Next, several committees were established to get the organization work under way: library (Beale, Mack, and Freund); temporary and permanent quarters (Beale); correspondence and publicity (Beale and Freund); admission (Freund and Lee); and securing lawyers for lectures (Beale and Mack).[53] Finally it was determined that a faculty of law and politics was to be established to have charge of the prelaw studies and postgraduate studies. The faculty would consist of the entire faculty of law and designated members of the Historical Group of Departments (philosophy, political economy, political science, history, and sociology). All of these areas would require much to be done before October 1, and the faculty proceeded to the tasks at hand.

5   "Pure Law" versus "The Whole Field of Man as a Social Being"

As the recruitment of faculty continued in the spring of 1902, Harper, Beale, Freund, and Mack turned to establishing the curriculum. Harper had insisted that legal education at Chicago was to extend beyond the curricula of the foremost law schools and involve the related sciences of history, economics, and philosophy. Further, Harper maintained, legal education was to do more than meet the demands of a particular state accrediting agency. Students were to be educated for careers other than that of private practice. The question of law-related studies had been posed earlier at Harvard and Columbia, and the result had been the exclusion of such courses from law school curricula. But the European system, and the German universities in particular, were to have great influences at Chicago. Thus the traditional Harvard notion of "pure law" was to be influenced by German legal education and mix with the emerging social sciences at Chicago to have a significant impact on the definition of American legal education.

The German Influence
Law-Related Courses

At the 1902 spring convocation Harper brought the university community up-to-date on the organization of the school. The faculty had been completely hired. Harper announced in accordance with the wish of the trustees that these men should for the most part give full-time to teaching. Harper observed that this policy, which ran contrary to the existing practices of the time, presented problems, since the number of people who had prepared themselves for the law-teaching profession was small. Harper wanted to break the tradition of a part-time faculty comprising men whose teaching responsibilities were secondary to other professional responsibilities. He also wanted faculty who had first-hand familiarity with the practice of law as well as proven experience as law professors. And despite the paucity of outstanding law professors, Harper told his audience, the new faculty was a distinguished one and worthy of the colleagues already enticed to the new university.[1]

But the highlight of Harper's speech to the university community at the spring convocation in 1902 involved the proposed curriculum of the school, which would emphasize "the study of law in its larger historical relations."[2] Chicago's curriculum would extend beyond not only the curricula of the numerous proprietary law schools across the country but beyond those of the foremost law schools.

Accepting the notion initially stated with such force by Christopher Columbus Langdell that the study of the law be scientific, Harper further insisted that legal education involve the related sciences of history, economics, and philosophy. The study of law had to consider man as part of the social milieu in which he existed. To train a person simply for admission to the bar was not enough.

> A University School of Law is far more than a training institute for admission to the bar. It implies a scientific knowledge of law and of legal and juristic methods. But these are the crystallization of ages of human progress. They cannot be understood in their entirety without a clear comprehension of the historic forces of which they are the product, and of the social environment with which they are in living contact. A scientific study of law involves the related sciences of history, economics, philosophy—the whole field of man as a social being.[3]

The curriculum that was drawn up immediately at Chicago departed in some degree from the accepted models, and as the early years passed at Chicago Harper's larger notion of legal education served as a guiding principle for the development of the Law School.

Harper's opinions on the proper curriculum ran contrary to those maintained at Harvard and the other law schools. The question of training men for careers other than that of private practice, such as in government, business, or teaching, and of how these careers related to the study of law, had come up earlier at Harvard and Columbia. John W. Burgess had been brought to Columbia to revive the instruction at the college level in the social sciences that Francis Lieber had initiated before he was fired by President Frederick A. P. Barnard. The subjects taught by Burgess were optional for law studies and were not a part of the law curriculum. In 1878 he began his campaign to expand the work in political science and constitutional and comparative law within the Law School. The formidable Theodore W. Dwight, whose authoritative leadership shaped Columbia Law School for over thirty years, resisted Burgess. In 1880 Burgess withdrew from the law faculty, and the trustees authorized an independent School of Political Science whose curriculum included Roman law, administrative law, and government. The law curriculum at Columbia and the traditions inherent in the Dwight method remained intact.[4]

Dean Ames at Harvard in 1900 also resisted the notion of incorporating political science courses into the curriculum of the Law School. In a letter to Eliot, Ames outlined his reluctance to comply with Eliot's proposal that political sciences be incorporated into the law curriculum. First, Ames argued that a new degree would be necessary, "for our present degree would be obviously unsuitable." Furthermore, Ames explained, "our present Faculty would have little or nothing to do with the new class of students. Indeed Professor Strobel and Professor Thayer are probably the only ones whom these students would care to hear." Ames was persuaded that a political science student would have no interest in private law. He maintained that a student would have trouble mastering the law as taught at Harvard unless he was completely immersed in legal education; the pursuit of other, unrelated studies would be a hindrance. The new curriculum would necessitate a new faculty. "This new group of teachers," Ames predicted, "would have very little to do with the men who are fitting themselves to be practitioners of law. There would be, therefore, very little in common between the present Law Faculty and the new teachers, and also very little cooperation between the two classes of students."[5]

The inclusion of political science courses in the Harvard Law

School was viewed by the law faculty as a move that would
have major consequences for the curriculum, faculty, students,
and indeed the entire spirit of the place. Ames declared to Eliot
that the law faculty would not allow the proposed new professors a voice in shaping the LL.B. curriculum and would
show little, if any, interest in the curriculum leading to the
degree in political science. In defense of Ames it should be
said that he was expressing opinions that were undoubtedly
held by the entire faculty. Ames saw Eliot's notion as merely
an "annex" to the Law School that would not add any prestige
to the school. The solution, maintained Ames, in accordance
with the Columbia precedent, was the creation of a new faculty
of political science.[6]

At Chicago the issue of law-related studies was posed and
resolved differently. As already pointed out, two political
scientists, Freund and Judson, had exercised major influence
on the preliminary plans for the Law School. Moreover, the
traditions that separated legal education from the emerging
social sciences and that played crucial roles in sustaining the
format of legal education at Columbia and Harvard were not
to provide major barriers at Chicago. As a new institution
Harper's university could either accept, reject, or modify the
existing trends in legal education and make new proposals.
Established as a graduate institution, the University of Chicago had strong roots in the English and European systems,
particularly in the German universities. Storr, in describing
the early faculty of the university, noted that "European modes
of education and investigation had become known to a significant fraction of the professoriate at first hand; but the greater
number of such models as the degrees of Faculty members
represented lay at a shorter distance to the East."[7] Freund, of
course, had received his legal training in Germany. Mack and
Lee had been introduced first-hand to the European system.
Beale, Hall, Whittier, and Mechem had no direct experience
with the continental universities.

As the European system and the German universities in
particular were to have great influence at Chicago, their major
characteristics should be noted briefly. The German system
placed greater demands on students than the most rigorous
American law schools. The law was not considered an area

separate from other disciplines and was taught as a part of the liberal arts. The German universities were communities of scholars as well as teaching institutions. Thus, Max Rheinstein observes, "they have not only the task of handing down from generation to generation the learning and wisdom of the past, and of increasing it through new creative thought and exploration, but also of preparing young men for practical professions."[8]

The study of law was connected to the arts and sciences. Before a European student could begin his legal education, a liberal arts education was essential. An applicant had to be a graduate of a gymnasium that had a nine-year course of study. An earned degree in the faculty of letters, arts, or sciences was required before a student could receive a law degree from a university. Admission was controlled by the law faculties, and the criteria for selection focused on the applicant's ability and achievements.

A doctorate in law in Germany followed three years of full-time residence. At the University of Berlin in the 1880s, approximately sixty courses of lectures in law were offered each semester by about twenty different instructors, with an average of three hours each week for each course. At Leipzig the curriculum was approximately the same but the faculty was smaller. As it was impossible for a student to attend all the lectures, a student would usually go to three or four daily, selected from twenty-five or thirty offerings. There were no separate buildings for the law schools, and all faculties of the university were housed under the same roof.

Under Imperial law all applicants to the bar had to study law in a university for at least three and a half years, and at least one-half of that time had to be spent in a German university. Since all universities were state-controlled, the courses were regulated by the government. It is interesting to observe, that, contrary to the practice in American legal education, there was no outlined curriculum in law in the German universities. The curriculum prescribed by the government covered civil, criminal, administrative, and constitutional law. The student was given a list of subjects to be studied at will in his preparation for the final examination.[9]

Another significant difference in the German model was the

Thomas M. Hoyne (Chicago Historical Society)

Joseph Henry Beale, Jr.

William Rainey Harper

Floyd Russell Mechem

James Parker Hall

Ernst Freund

Julian Mack (Chicago Historical Society)

The Midway Plaisance in 1893 during the Columbian Exposition, looking west. The Laird Bell Law Quadrangle was built on the site behind the Ferris wheel, which stood at the corner of Sixtieth Street and Woodlawn Avenue.

The Law School Building, circa 1903, looking southeast across the Midway.

John D. Rockefeller, Sr.

ALL READY FOR JOHN D. SANTA CLAUS AT THE UNIVERSITY OF CHICAGO.

DR. HARPER—"NOW, DON'T LOOK, CHILDREN, AND PERHAPS SANTA CLAUS WILL BRING US A NICE PRESENT."

This cartoon appeared in the *Chicago Record Herald* for December 2, 1902.

The Press Building, on the northwest corner of Ellis Avenue and Fifty-eighth Street, the first home of the Law School (1902–4).

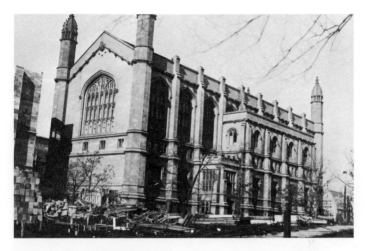

The Law School Building shortly after completion in 1904.

Theodore Roosevelt, after receiving the honorary degree of Doctor of Laws, at the laying of the cornerstone for the new Law School Building on April 2, 1903.

Fifty-seventh Street at the Illinois Central tracks in Hyde Park, circa 1893.

Washington Street in the Loop, looking west from Dearborn Street, circa 1893 (From *Chicago 1892*, Chicago Historical Society).

Sophonisba Breckenridge

The Law School Building, date unknown.

All photos, unless otherwise noted, are by courtesy of the Special Collections Department, Regenstein Library, University of Chicago.

important institution of *Achtenversendung,* or the migration
of law professors from one faculty to another. Moreover, the
professors had regular contact with all aspects of everyday
legal practice. Teaching law was recognized as a profession,
and professors were also judges, legal advisers, and scholars.
A distinguished law professor would write influential books,
be frequently cited as an authority, create and elaborate on
legal theories, and attempt to adapt law to changing circumstances in society.

The law teaching profession was controlled tightly from
within. To become a *Venia legendi,* one had to be a doctor and
write a dissertation. The first position was that of *Privatdozent*
and allowed the person to lecture in a particular field without
salary; the income for the aspiring professor came from the
lecture fees of the students the person was able to attract. One
became a salaried professor when an application to the minister of education was approved, following consultation with the
law faculty. After this point substance and methodology were
left to the law professors, and there were no limits to the freedom of academic teaching. "That the system left room for creative opposition and innovation," Rheinstein concludes, "was
the very basis of the brilliant position of the German universities in the world of scholarship and learning."[10]

The German influence on American legal education made
itself felt slowly. Certainly the range of scholarly interests and
writings of a Joseph Kohler were not characteristic of American law professors of the time. When Kohler received an
honorary degree of Doctor of Laws from the University of
Chicago in 1904, the breadth of the German scholar's career
was indicated by James Parker Hall:

> The field of his professional activity is almost as wide as
> the field of law itself. The index of his published writings
> lends itself to classification under most of the principal
> headings of a digest. He has written upon the law of
> contract, of property, of family rights, of succession, and of
> competition; upon commercial, maritime, and insurance
> law; upon patents, copyright, and trademarks; upon crimi-
> nal law and bankruptcy; upon both civil and criminal
> procedure, and upon public and administrative law; and he

has published numerous studies of the laws of ancient and half-civilized peoples, and of the history and philosophy of law in general.[11]

The German system, requiring a rigorous liberal arts background, emphasizing the relation of the law to other disciplines, and producing law professors with academic and research interests, influenced not only the curriculum at Chicago but the spirit of the school—a spirit which was initiated and sustained by Harper as he had done throughout the organization of the university.

Law-Related Courses and "Pure Law"

The University Senate approved a basic curriculum for the Law School on March 1, 1902, before the arrangement had been made with Harvard to secure Beale and before the rest of the original faculty had been recruited. After approving the name of the school—"The School of Law and Jurisprudence" —the senate recommended a curriculum which would cover one year of preliminary studies and a three-year "course of technical law studies." The professional course of study was to "cover the subjects enumerated in the Rules of the Supreme Court of Illinois, real and personal property, personal rights, contracts, evidence, common law and equity pleading, partnership, bailments, negotiable instruments, principal and agent, principal and surety, domestic relations, wills, corporations, equity jurisprudence, criminal law, and the principles of the Constitution of the State and the United States, and legal ethics." As admission to the bar of Illinois was controlled by the Supreme Court of Illinois, such a statement was in order. The guiding hand of Freund is evident, however, for the statement continued by stating that other subjects could be added, including public and private international law, admiralty, federal law, jurisprudence, and procedure.[12]

Thus, even before the faculty existed, a definition of legal education had been provided by the university authorities, stimulated by Harper, Freund, and Judson. To a limited extent, students would be able to pursue studies that were not strictly of a professional character and were not required for admission to the bar. Emphasis was to be placed on the opportunities for future graduates of the school who planned to enter government work or fields other than that of private practice. "As many lawyers enter public life, and by reason of their technical knowledge have in many respects a contracting influence upon the framing of laws, they should be enabled to study principles of legislation as well as principles of law." For this purpose, the senate said, "the work of the Law School will be affiliated with the work of the departments of Political Economics, Political Science, and Sociology, and of the College of Commerce and Administration."[13]

The university's Department of Political Economy included James Lawrence Laughlin, Adolph Miller, and a young assistant professor, Thorstein B. Veblen. Courses offered in political economy that were related to the law included the relation of the state to industrial organization; trusts, taught by Miller; a course on the origin of present forms of industry, taught by Veblen; finance, including the study of taxation, offered by Miller; comparative railway legislation, taught by William Hill; and the history of commerce, conducted by Henry Rand Hatfield. The principal officers of instruction in political science were Harry Pratt Judson, Edmund James, Ernst Freund, and Charles E. Merriam.

In the political science curriculum many courses and seminars were taught that were related to the law, at least as envisioned by Harper, Freund, Judson, and the University Senate: federal government, federal constitutional law, municipal government, and the law of municipal corporations. Under a section of the political science curriculum called "jurisprudence," courses taught by Freund included institutes of Roman law; history and elements of the law of property (based on the Second Book of Blackstone's *Commentaries*); criminal law; elements of jurisprudence, which concentrated on fundamental legal ideas and principles illustrated by cases and statutes; and the law of persons. Several courses in the Department of Sociology, chaired by Albion W. Small, were related to the law, as well as several in the College of Commerce and Administration.

Having in mind many of the courses taught in these several departments on the Midway, Freund insisted that law had been taught at Chicago long before the formal establishment of the Law School. His interest in seeing a separate Law School created, even one fashioned after the standard Harvard model, was strengthened by his conviction that the university already had a rich curriculum that could supplement conventional legal education.

The curriculum adopted by the law faculty on April 15, upon recommendation of the Curriculum Committee composed of Beale, Hall, and Whittier, included a prescribed first year which was similar to the traditional model. Whittier would teach contracts; Hall, torts, using Ames and Smith's *Cases on Torts*; Beale, criminal law, using his own casebook; Freund, property, using Gray's *Cases on Property*; Freund would also teach persons, using Woodruff's *Cases on Domestic Relations*; Whittier would conduct pleading; and Hall would teach agency, using Wambaugh's casebook. The work of the second and third years was to be elective and interchangeable, with the exception of certain courses to be designated that could not be taken before the third year. Here there were significant departures from the Harvard model. In addition to the standard curriculum, courses and seminars could be elected in administrative law, municipal corporations, federal jurisdiction and practice, international law, Roman law, and legal ethics.[14] After the arrival of Mechem, students could elect to take public officers. Once established at the University of Chicago Law School, courses in principles of legislation, administrative law, international law, Roman and civil law, comparative law, and systematic and comparative jurisprudence became part of the law curricula.

The practical component in traditional legal education was not ignored in the early curriculum at Chicago despite the fact that it was overshadowed by the controversy concerning the role of law-related courses vis-à-vis the traditional "pure law." Blewett Lee had long been an advocate for teaching practice in law schools. In a speech before the legal education section of the American Bar Association in 1896, Lee cited figures from a recent study of the decisions in the appellate courts in the country which revealed that, in half the cases tried, the lawyers were unable to bring before the court the merits of the cases. Thus, suggested Lee, this fact signified "that in the actual administration of justice in America today, a knowledge of procedure is worth as much to the practitioner as his knowledge of all the rest of the law put together." Lee denounced the opinion that lawyers had to pick up their technical knowledge "in the hard school of experience." The law schools, Lee suggested, could do something to cope with the problem. "We are apt to forget that while law is a science, practising law is an art, and we might as well expect to make a man a civil engineer in a closet, as to make him a lawyer by only having him read books."[15]

Lee, however, did not subscribe to the notion that a law office, even a good city office, was a suitable place to learn practice. "Except in the smallest offices, the work is specialized by division of labor to an extent which prevents the young law clerk from acquiring any general familiarity with practice. The members of the firm have no time to instruct or correct him." Lee, who insisted that a law school had to be national in character, noted that students would practice in many different jurisdictions. A thorough understanding of procedure was therefore imperative. "Procedure is the skeleton of our jurisprudence," Lee maintained. "When we dispense with the study of common law procedure, we shall dispense with the knowledge of the common law." Confronting directly the notion held by some educators that a practical education was a contradiction in terms, Lee suggested that more was needed than an imaginative statement in a law school catalogue. "The chief object of teaching is to make a man who can do things he has not been taught how to do."[16]

Without questioning the theory that law professors should be full-time teachers, Lee did urge faculty to keep in touch with the bar. For Lee it was not a question of either practical education or theoretical instruction: "the grandeur is in the faithful teaching rather than the imposing topic, and it is the little details which make the great lawyers." The lawyer "who goes forth to his life work trained in the technical details of his profession, need not lose the scholarship which has made our calling illustrious."[17] Consistent with this opinion expressed by his colleague, Whittier taught the required courses at Chicago on pleading, although illness was to limit his teaching. Harper too did not want a separation to occur between the school and the bar and thus allowed Julian Mack to combine his practice with teaching. Eventually Mack would serve as a distinguished judge in several courts, while remaining a member of the faculty.

Harper also hired a well-known practicing attorney, Horace Kent Tenney, as professor of law on a part-time basis. Tenney, who grew up in Chicago, attended the preparatory department of the old University of Chicago but received his A.B. from the University of Vermont. He was graduated from Wisconsin Law School in 1881. The senior partner in the Chicago firm of Tenney, McConnell, Coffeen and Harding, Tenney had lectured on practice at John Marshall Law School. His elective practice course at Chicago included study of the nature and jurisdiction of the courts, venue of actions, proceedings, filing and service of pleadings; proceedings on default, assessment of damages, appearance, demurrers, pleadings to merits, and set-off and recoupment.

Although the alteration of the standard curriculum by the inclusion of courses not considered "pure law" that occurred in the early years of the Law School merits attention, this innovation did not change drastically the major function of legal education: to prepare lawyers for private practice. In his formal announcement of the school in October 1902, Harper described the faculty, curriculum, and the objectives. The course of study, he observed, was "largely determined by the historical development of the common law and by the legal requirements for admission to the practice of law."[18]

In documents written in 1905, in the course of an administrative battle between the central administration and the law faculty over issues involving credits, the position of the faculty as they put together the curriculum in the spring and summer of 1902 is further explained.[19] In defense of their position that certain law courses should not be given as majors, the faculty began by stating that "the object of the Law School is primarily *professional* education, the effective training of men for actual practice—not merely such general culture as can be obtained from fragments of legal study." The study of law, suggested the faculty, was divided into various subjects "based upon natural groups of related principles that had been recognized by courts, writers, and law teachers." The casebooks, prepared to correspond to the recognized organization, must be used in order that students "acquire the accurate, detailed, technical knowledge necessary for a thorough professional education." The problem of coverage within the curriculum and thoroughness of instruction was central since the content of many subjects could not adequately be treated in the time available for one major. Furthermore, the faculty insisted that three years did not allow enough time to cover the material: "Though some subjects could not well be contracted, all might be treated in greater detail, were this not at the expense of reducing the variety of subjects that could be taken by a student in three years." In concluding their argument, the faculty reminded the University Council that "the matters discussed in this paper were all considered three years ago when the Law School was established, were explained to the satisfaction of President Harper, and the present arrangement was adopted with his approval as the best practicable working system."[20] Thus the primary function of the school, reflected in the basic curriculum, was the preparation of lawyers.

The work load of the faculty, after they had spent many hours in organizing the school, was a heavy one. At Chicago each faculty member had to teach four or five subjects for a total of eight hours a week; at Harvard three subjects was the maximum for a total of six hours. The quarter system created more examinations to be given and graded. "In coming to a new School it has been necessary for most of us to give up some familiar courses and undertake others, in order to arrange the work to the best advantage. It takes a few years to get a new course into good teachable condition, and in addition the teacher must keep up to date in four or five subjects on which 60 courts of record in America alone, besides those of the British Empire, are daily pouring out decisions."[21]

Harper's Summer Session and the Law School

One of Harper's innovations in American higher education was the introduction of the quarter system. Students could, if they chose, attend the university throughout the year thus decreasing the total time spent in pursuing a program. The Law School was not to be excepted from this format. The law faculty supported the notion of a summer session from the beginning for at least two reasons. First, because of the small size of the faculty, the additional session enabled the school to offer a more diverse curriculum than would have been possible within the traditional academic year. Second, the summer session brought to the Law School a steady stream of the best law teachers in the United States. During the early years Chicago would enrich its curriculum by recruiting distinguished faculty for its summer sessions: Bruce Wyman, James Taylor Burcham, Edwin Hamlin Woodruff, Nathan Abbott, Emlin McClain, Horace Lafayette Wilgus, Walter Wheeler Cook, Harold Dexter Hazeltine, Edward Sampson Thurston, Henry Moore Bates, Wesley Newcomb Hohfeld, and Roscoe Pound, to name but a few.[22]

The faculty who were recruited the first year to supplement the permanent faculty further allowed Harper to bridge the gap between the theoretical and the practical. Henry Varnum Freeman, lecturer on legal ethics, was presiding justice of the Appellate Court, First District of Illinois. A graduate of Yale, he had practiced in Chicago until 1893 when he was nominated for judge of the Superior Court, and he had lectured on medical jurisprudence at Rush Medical College in 1898. The lecturer on admiralty law, Charles Edward Kremer, had the largest admiralty practice in Chicago and the Northwest for over twenty years. A product of the apprenticeship system, Kremer had lectured in maritime law and admiralty practice at the Chicago College of Law. Harper selected one of the university's trustees, Francis Warner Parker, to be lecturer in patent law. Another product of the apprenticeship system, Parker had served as an examiner in the Patent Office in Washington for several years before returning to Chicago in 1884 to practice law.

To complete the ranks of lecturers, Harper recruited four more men who also combined experience with teaching. George R. Peck had practiced law until 1874 when he was appointed United States attorney by President Grant. He returned to private practice until he became general solicitor of the Atchison, Topeka and Santa Fe Railway Company. In 1892 he came to Chicago and became general counsel for the Milwaukee and St. Paul Railway and senior partner in the law firm of Peck, Miller and Starr. Frank Fremont Reed was graduated from Michigan and then came to Chicago in 1882 where he practiced law. For five years prior to the Chicago appointment he had been the nonresident lecturer on copyright and trademark law at Michigan as well as at the Chicago College of Law. John Zane was also a Michigan graduate and had returned to Salt Lake City where he became assistant United States attorney of Utah, served as reporter of the Supreme Court of Utah, and also practiced law. He came to Chicago in 1899 to practice law and published *Banks and Banking* in 1900.

The most eminent lecturer, however, was Samuel Williston, professor of law at Harvard. Williston, a good friend and colleague of Beale, was the first of many respected law professors to visit Chicago. A graduate of Harvard College and Harvard Law School cum laude in 1884, he served as secretary to Justice Horace Gray before practicing in Boston. He joined the Harvard faculty in 1890 and over a period of fifteen years was a prolific writer and editor, his works including *Parsons on Contracts* (1893); *Cases on Contracts* (1894); *Cases on Sales* (1894); *Stephen on Pleading* (1895); and *Cases on Bankruptcy*. The Williston appointment was typical of those that would increasingly bring distinguished faculty to Chicago during the summer sessions. Edward H. Levi has suggested that this means of attracting notables to teach for one quarter "may have made up for the apparent unwillingness or inability of the School for many years to attract or to keep bright young teachers."[23] In any case, the roster of the summer school faculty would continue to be an eminent and diverse one for many years.

At their November 7 meeting, the faculty voted to provide instruction for beginning students in the summer quarter of 1903 by offering full courses in contracts and torts and by teaching three majors of elective work. Beale would teach damages; Freund, conveyancing; and Mack, trusts. Although the program was designed as a three-year course of study, a student could obtain a degree in a shorter length of time by going throughout the year. This possibility served to combat one of the major criticisms of the three-year program that many law schools were to adopt after Chicago, that is, of the economic hardship and delayed entry to the bar resulting from the three-year program.[24]

By the second summer session, 50 percent of the law students were to take advantage of the extra quarter. According to
Hall, this indicated clearly that there was a strong demand
for the additional quarter "on the part of men as mature and
capable as those constituting our student body." Furthermore,
Hall contended, the summer quarter "is a practical step toward
the desideratum of getting young men into their professional
work at as early an age as is consistent with thorough preparation."[25] Compared with students in other departments of the
university, approximately 50 percent more law students pursued work throughout the year. The importance of the summer
session in relation to the curriculum continued to increase, and
two years later Hall reported that almost every law student
took more work than was required for the degree and that one-
fourth of the students remained more than nine quarters in
residence. Hall suggested that the growing complexity of the
law and the proliferation of studies related to the study of law
increasingly made three years of legal education insufficient:

> It is becoming more evident that three years is a short
> time to spend upon the systematic study of law as a prepara-
> tion for practice. The constant widening horizon of human
> activity compels a corresponding development and refine-
> ment of legal principles, and what today seems simple
> rapidly becomes a matter for the specialist. The principal
> objection to increasing the time of study required in our
> leading law schools is that it still further postpones an
> entrance upon practice perhaps in many cases too long
> delayed to take full advantage of the plasticity of early
> manhood.[26]

Harper's Hopes for Prelaw
Study Are Realized

In directing the fundamental policy for the organization of the
Law School, the trustees had voted unanimously that the school
"should be essentially a graduate school, its regular students
being required to have the Bachelor's degree, or at least three
years of work in an approved college."[27] The professional curriculum at the Law School was designed as a graduate-level

program in accordance with Harper's opinions and the general design of the university. From the earliest discussions on the Law School Harper had insisted that a prelaw program be available. In the provisional statement adopted by the Senate on March 1, 1902, Harper's hopes were supported. "The preliminary course in the first year of the Senior Year," the statement explained, "is intended to direct the College work of those who expect to devote themselves to law, to studies which without being technical are related to jurisprudence or are otherwise of especial value or interest to the future lawyer. These courses will include English and American Constitutional History, Political Economy, and other related subjects."[28]

The law faculty, once organized, concurred with Harper's objectives. Having decided on the professional curriculum at their first meeting, the faculty agreed to take charge of the prelegal studies. The next day they designated one faculty member each from the departments of philosophy, political economy, political science, history, and sociology to serve as the Faculty of Law and Politics. The curriculum was to include two majors each of English constitutional history, political economy, American constitutional history, and three majors to be selected from a list of courses to be designated by a committee consisting of Freund, Laughlin, and Jameson. The faculty also instructed that the Law Circular contain recommendations to the students entering the Law School from other colleges to pursue studies similar to those in Chicago's prelaw curriculum.[29] Harper's ulterior motive in urging a prelaw program was his hope that the college program would be shortened, not by creating a three-year college program, but by dropping a year from high school, thus enabling students to finish their college and law programs in six years.

Harper's opinions on the prelaw program and its relation to the traditional college programs were expressed in a speech given before the regents of the State University of New York on June 27, 1899. Harper criticized the waste in higher education, in particular the preparation for professional and graduate study provided by colleges. As originator of the junior college movement, Harper felt that the first two years of college should be a continuation of high school work. The influence of the German system was evident in his belief that the

length of time should be shortened in preparatory education.
Thus Harper asserted:

> The only redeeming element in the situation is found in
> the fact that by the present methods of preliminary educa-
> tion so much time is exhausted that many of the students
> who enter college have reached an age when even in the
> freshman and sophomore years they are capable of doing
> work of a higher order. But this, when it occurs, is at the
> cost of professional training, in later years of life or at the
> cost of years which should have been used in a different
> way.[30]

Harper was against those who favored a three-year college and
was unhappy with the failure of educators to see the difference
between college and university methods.

For Harper university education meant graduate education.
The college curricula of his time did not respond to the current
demands of professional education, which had changed over
the decades. Harper's plan called for four years of high school
(the last two to be considered junior college) and two years
of senior college, which would include preprofessional education. The three-year college course ignored what Harper
called the cultural value of the subject matter in the first part
of professional training. In a speech to the National Education
Association given the summer following the Law School's first
year, Harper declared: "I can conceive no work more valuable
to a young man or woman than the first year in the curriculum
of the law, the medical, or the divinity school, or in the school
of education. The fact that the method in the professional
schools is different from that in the college is, in the majority of
cases, a distinct advantage, and in no case an injury, since it
serves as a corrective of a tendency toward dilettantism unquestionably encouraged by the more lax methods of the later
years of college work."[31]

A three-year college program advocated by other educators
during this time subordinated the college almost completely to
the professional school. Harper would not subscribe to that
principle. "It is largely because of the increased demands for
the professional schools that it seems necessary to shorten the
college course. This does not seem to be in harmony," Harper

suggested, "with the fact that a comparatively small number
of students really expect to enter professional schools."[32]

Charles W. Eliot, as is evident from his paper read to the
same National Education Association meeting, did not agree
with Harper's opinions on the role of collegiate education in
relation to professional study. Eliot was against the disappear-
ance of the B.A. degree. He supported a three-year college program only if the same work was covered in three years as in
a four-year program. He agreed with Harper that a college
degree was a desirable prerequisite for law school but did not
allow for the flexibility of Harper, who was willing to accept
qualified students after three years in his junior college/senior
college scheme. Eliot admitted that his objection was "senti-
mental" and suggested that other "private-venture" schools
in the large cities could absorb the "young men of remarkable
powers who have had no opportunities in their earlier years
to obtain a good, systematic education."[33] Ames agreed with
Eliot on this point and indeed may have been the major influence on him. Beale, after returning to Harvard from Chicago,
did not agree with Eliot. In a letter to Eliot he wrote: "you will
notice that Harvard seems to stand alone in refusing to permit
the saving of a year, without extra work in the combined college and professional course."[34]

Columbia's Nicholas Murray Butler joined Eliot in urging
the retention of the B.A. degree: it should "be preserved at all
hazards as an initial part of our educational organization. It is
distinctively American and a very powerful factor in upbuild-
ing of the nation's culture and idealism. It should be treated as
a thing of value in itself and for itself, and not merely as an
incident to graduate study or to professional schools."[35] But
Butler went beyond Eliot and maintained that there should be
no preprofessional courses in the B.A. program, and that a
separate two-year college course in liberal arts be established
for preprofessional training without a degree: "degrees are the
tinsel of higher education and not its reality." For Butler a B.A.
was not necessary for admission to law school for it "delays too
long entrance upon life-work and it does not use the time and
effort of the intending professional student to the best
advantage."[36]

Harper was, of course, the victor in regard to the format for preprofessional education at Chicago. Although his plan for separating the junior colleges from the university campus never materialized, he was able to initiate preprofessional programs beginning with the first year of senior college.[37] In prelaw the curriculum was devoted primarily to political economy and American and English constitutional history. The first *Annual Register* containing the Law School Announcements listed the "Prelegal Curriculum" which was "intended to direct the college work of those who expect to devote themselves to law, to studies which without being professional are related to jurisprudence, or are otherwise of especial value and interest to the future lawyer."[38]

In summarizing the results of establishing the prelegal curriculum, Hall alluded to the difficulties at other institutions and noted in a report to Harper that "the relation between the Colleges and the Law School, by which one year in the latter may be counted toward an academic degree from the former, has been adjusted as to secure a maximum of flexibility. . . . The Law Faculty wishes to express its appreciation and sympathy shown by the members of the Faculty of Arts and Sciences in the Senate in assenting to these arrangements— an attitude in marked contrast to that of the academic faculties of some of our sister institutions, whose law schools are endeavoring to secure a similar basis of cooperation."[39]

Thus the faculty were influenced by the German system of legal education as they put together a curriculum committed to the "whole field of man as a social being," a curriculum that extended beyond the "pure law" of the Harvard model. In particular the German emphasis on a rigorous liberal arts background, the relation of law to other disciplines, and law professors with strong academic and research interests would quickly become evident in Harper's law school. Other established programs in political economics, political science, sociology, and history at the university were to be utilized in the prelaw program. The practical orientation of traditional legal education was not ignored, as emphasis was placed on procedure courses and the maintenance of close relations with the practicing bar. The curriculum was to prepare lawyers not only for the practice of law but for other careers.

6　Last-Minute Tasks
A Library, Standards and Degrees, Students, and a Home

The first priorities for Harper had been to secure the best faculty available and then to define the curriculum. With these matters underway, the faculty had other tasks to pursue, with less than six months remaining before the opening of the Law School. Rockefeller's grant of $50,000 for the purchase of books had been generous; yet the problems of securing books and journals for what would eventually become one of the finest law libraries in the United States were numerous.

Of more significance in regard to Chicago's influence was the school's position on standards of admission and the awarding of the *Juris Doctor* degree. Amid these deliberations the faculty had to give attention to recruiting students and the location of the Law School. With October 1 rapidly approaching, the faculty, under the constant eye and with the strong support of Harper, tackled these jobs with great energy and imagination. The excitement of creating a new, innovative school had taken hold.

The Library
A Laboratory for Legal Education

Perhaps the most pressing problem confronting the faculty when they met for the first time, on April 15 at the Chicago Club, was that of the law library. The library, according to Beale's estimate in his March discussions with Harper, needed at least 20,000 volumes at the start. A major problem was the staff necessary for this monumental job of collecting a major library in little time. "Now to get together, or even make the beginning of getting together such a library by October would require the services of the Dean and, as it seemed to me," Beale

said, "of a librarian and two assistant librarians."[1] Harper
took the position that scholarship students could cover the
library desk and that assistant librarians were not needed, although additional help could be found if Beale insisted.

Beale relented and turned his attention to the identification
and location of books and materials. At their initial meeting
the faculty gave power to acquire these materials to a library
committee consisting of Beale, Mack, and Freund to act with
regard to the following kinds of material: "American and
English Reports; Canadian, Scotch, and Irish Reports; Cyclo-
paedias, Digest annotations, Collections of Cases, revised Statutes and Session Laws to date; Standard Legal periodicals; Text
Books."[2] The only existing law collection in the city of Chicago
of any merit was at the Law Institute, downtown in the County
Court House, but its usefulness to the university was impaired
by inadequacies in the collection and its location. Harper vis-
ualized the greatest law library in the West—if not in the
United States—and as usual was willing to pay for it. The task,
however, fell on the law faculty, who because of the market
were forced to turn to New York City, London, and Paris. With
the first day of classes six months away, the objective was an
ambitious one. The brunt of the responsibility fell on Beale
and Mack, who had the knowledge necessary for the selection
of books. All the faculty agreed that the initial library should
include "all material essential to the scholarly teaching of
English and American law, and a working library in the law
of a few important European countries."[3]

The relation of the library to the methods of teaching law
was important, as Beale emphasized: "The law, as a science,
must be taught by putting in the hands of students the sources
of knowledge, and following investigation and comparison, a
scientific judgment would be gradually formed." This method
of instruction, Beale observed, lent itself to the study of law,
and thus the importance of the law library could not be overemphasized.

All the objective sources of knowledge of it [the law] lie on
the printed page. The library is the laboratory of our science,
and a great law library affords all the material which the
student needs for his study. The task of the teacher is only

to form and direct his judgment and kindle his enthusiasm. The original sources of our law are the decisions of our courts, the official depositories of legal learning; and only by a study of these decisions can we know the law as a science.[4]

By the first day of classes nearly 18,000 volumes had been purchased. In a progress report to Harper on July 30 Mack noted that most of the books and sets had been ordered. He projected that the cost of the continuations of the various series of reports and periodicals would be about $1,500 annually and tactfully stated that the faculty had proceeded on the basis that the appropriations for books in future years would be made in the same manner. Mack informed Harper that it had been the hope of the faculty that a reserve of $5,000 out of the $50,000 could be held back for future emergencies. Yet the task of building the library, even under the guidance of experienced men, had already resulted in financial problems. "We find, however, that emergencies have already arisen since we entered our main contracts and that we can, at the present time, secure some desirable things at a lower price than we can hope to purchase them for in the future."[5] Thus the reserve anticipated by the faculty had dwindled to $2,500, which Mack observed would be exhausted when the proposed Reading Room had become available for students.

The problems in purchasing the books were compounded by bureaucratic problems within the institution. All orders for books had to be approved by the university librarian, who then sent the request to the Committee on Expenditures, which had been created early in 1897 after representatives of Rockefeller voiced concern over the annual deficit situation and the internal inadequacies of the supervision of the budget. Upon approval by that committee, the university press ordered the books, catalogued them when they came in, and then sent them to the Law School. The system was cumbersome. First, the element of time was crucial; second, Mack and Beale frequently wished to order editions of books not acceptable to the university librarian or the Committee on Expenditure because similar books could be purchased for less. Freund attempted to resolve the conflict by making several recommendations to Harper in midsummer, in order to facilitate the attempts to buy books that were being made, and the tension was slightly eased.[6]

The conflict involving the law library also affected other university policies. After reviewing the current rules in *The Register* on his way home to Cambridge after the first faculty planning session, Beale told Harper that exceptions would have to be made for the professional libraries and that the law library should not be seen as a regular departmental library. "The law library is distinctly a workshop, and should perhaps be treated rather like a laboratory than like a departmental library." The regulations for the departmental libraries would not apply. For instance, the rule that departmental libraries should be closed at six o'clock would prevent evening study by law students; the rules for supervision would also require modification. "I suggest that libraries of the professional schools of divinity, law and medicine should be treated as in a separate class," Beale argued, "rules for them being formulated after we have had a little experience."[7] Harper responded that he saw no problem in making arrangements for the law library under the regulations of the departmental libraries. "Many of the departmental libraries are kept open until ten o'clock," Harper told Beale. "I think we can make such adjustments as are necessary without making a new division, but I shall be glad to have you prepare all the suggestions you can think of on this subject."[8]

Other university regulations annoyed Beale as he attempted to tie up loose ends from Cambridge. Harper questioned him on several of his last-minute decisions, and Beale submitted a written statement of the difficulties justifying the decisions that "we have thought ourselves obliged to meet by action outside the regular rules." The issues involved appear minor. The administration was upset with Beale for instructing the librarian, Frederick Schenk, to have the regular carpenter build a partition to assure privacy for the ladies' toilet room: "without waiting for a requisition, I told him and the carpenter that if necessary I would pay the bills myself." Beale, whose correspondence with Harper was always cordial, continued to defend his actions with an offhand criticism of the bureaucratic procedures at the university. "I think we have violated the rules in no other purchases of supplies. I cannot be sure," Beale commented cryptically, "since we have no copy of the rules and we get contradictory information from different administrative officers."[9]

The administration was also alarmed because the Law School had broken policies for receiving new books. Immediately before the beginning of school, many of the books were scattered about the Reading Room unprocessed by the press and thereby inaccessible to students and faculty. Beale had the books put in their proper places on the shelves before they were checked in officially by the press. "They will there be easier to check than before," Beale told Harper, "and the danger of double charge for the books is I hope not materially increased." Beale forewarned Harper that he planned to continue this procedure, as several thousands of the most important books had yet to arrive. Because of the time pressure, the books had been accepted without accession cards for them being made by the general library: "if we had waited for that, we might not have had our books this year." The law faculty was concerned that perforation, which was required as a matter of university policy, would lessen the value of the books if future exchange was necessary. "In these breaches," Beale suggested, "we have acted only in view of what seemed to us the absolute necessity of having all possible preparations made before the opening of school. Our equipment is necessarily imperfect even now."[10]

Beale was to find many of the Chicago administrative policies bothersome at times, perhaps because of the established practices, but also because his academic background had not included administrative experience. One reason, cited by Beale himself, was his familiarity with the looser Harvard procedures. Writing to Eliot one month after classes began, Beale acknowledged that the experiment was going well and that he and Mrs. Beale had been received with the greatest kindness. His occasional unhappiness with Harper's way of running the institution, however, came out: "I do feel, however, that there is too strong a tendency to get up machinery just for the sake of seeing the wheels go 'round. To one trained under the simple but effectual rules of Harvard, practices here seem needlessly complicated." He did suggest to Eliot, however, that Harvard might consider one of Harper's features, "the Bureau of Information and Faculty Exchange, where all questions are answered, all communications between officers of the University are received and delivered, and an express telegraph and telephone office is maintained for the students."[11]

Despite the internal problems, the lack of a librarian, and the pressures of time, Beale, Mack, and Freund pulled together an exceptional law library over the summer. The collection was divided into five main groups: reports of cases; statutes; textbooks; periodicals; and trials, biographies, and legal miscellany. In regard to reports of cases, "the main repository of the common law," according to Hall in a later summary, they purchased a complete collection of authorities in American, English, Scotch, Irish, Canadian, Australian, New Zealand, higher Indian, as well as some recent South African reports. The last-named reports were significant because of the connection with the Roman-Dutch law. The Australian reports were important because the Australian colonies had been leading in some important branches of legislation. The American reports included the published decisions of all the federal and state courts, superior and inferior, except a few series of Pennsylvania county court decisions. The reports were accompanied by digests that gave clues to the cases and made them available for use. The collection of statutes included all English, Irish, Scotch, and Canadian statutes, and the session laws for all American states and Canadian provinces. The statutory law was divided into codes and statutory revisions, and the annual session laws of the different legislative bodies.[12]

The collection of codes and revisions, together with the session laws which were subsequently passed, made it possible to ascertain the existing statutory law of every English-speaking jurisdiction. The interest in the session laws was partly practical, insofar as they explained earlier decisions, and to a greater extent historical, as they illustrated the development of legislation. In regard to treatises, the library had all American and English treatises of any practical value and a large number of old English treatises of historical importance. All law periodicals in English had been obtained in complete sets.

Special purchases, classified as legal miscellany, were made, including a complete set of the Old Bailey and Central Sessions cases that contained the records of English criminal trials for nearly two centuries. There were also volumes on important English and American trials which, combined with the Old Bailey and Central Sessions cases, created a distinctive collection for the study of crime, criminal psychology, and social conditions. Several collector's items had been purchased, among others several rare volumes of early Illinois laws and Pope's compilation of 1815. The purchases also included a working library in French, German, Spanish, and Mexican law and a complete set of the Patent Office Reports and the *Patent Office Gazette* from the beginning. The first contribution to the Law School library took the form of two books donated by Julius Rosenthal, who had helped found the library of the Law Institute and later became a trustee of the university: *Origines Juridiciales; or Historical Memorials of the English Law Courts of Justice* (1680) by Sir William Drydale, and *Dionysii Halicarnassei Antiquitatum Romanorum* (1546). This philanthropy was later reciprocated in a sense by Julian Mack, who upon the death of his close friend established the Julius Rosenthal Loan Fund.[13]

The securing of a collection which became, practically overnight, one of the greatest law libraries was done largely without the services of a law librarian. In March Beale had told Harper that the "appointment of librarian ought certainly to be the first business." At that time Beale suggested a candidate: "I have had in mind but one man in the country, I might say in the world, for your purpose, if he can be had: that is, Mr. C. C. Soule, the president of the Boston Book Company, whose work in legal bibliography is the best that has been done in this country or in England. I think the librarian would have to go to London and to Paris for you as soon as may be."[14] There is no indication that Harper made any effort to secure Soule.

Instead Beale brought with him from Harvard Frederick William Schenk, who had been a cataloguer in the Harvard Law Library for two years. His departure was not a matter of much concern to Harvard, as Ames wrote to Eliot: "Mr. Schenck [sic], one of the assistants in the cataloging work, has left to go to Chicago. I am quite willing to give him up to

Beale, not valuing him very highly for our own work."[15] At
Chicago he became a valuable person, as a memorandum from
Hall to Harper, after Schenk had been there two years, shows.
In urging a salary increase from $900 to $1,200 Hall said: "He
is a very capable man, married, and is worth the increased
amount. It would be very difficult to get a man with his special
knowledge about law books, prices, and cataloguing for the
money elsewhere."[16]

Thus Beale, Mack, Freund, and Schenk put together a library
of over 18,000 volumes in less than six months. In the first
Announcements of the Law School mention was made of the
extraordinary effort: "The School has acquired an adequate
library of about eighteen thousand volumes, an equipment, it is
believed, superior to that of any other law school in the
West."[17] Reference was then made to the general and departmental libraries of the university, which contained approximately 350,000 volumes. The *Announcements* for the second
year gave a more detailed description of the collection with
a prefatory note that the acquisition of this great law library
was necessary because the faculty and students were expected
"to carry on their work on the University grounds independently of the library of the Law Institute in the County Court
House—a year ago the only well-furnished law library in the
city of Chicago."[18] Harper's desire for a great law library had
been accomplished in short order: a fact of some irony, for
one of Harper's greatest failures as president of the university
involved his attempts to secure a good university librarian and
to organize a general library to match the calibre of the other
components of the university.[19]

Standards for Admission
and the J.D. Degree

On October 1, 1902, the first day of classes for Harper's law
school, the student newspaper noted: "The University of Chicago Law School is the first to offer the degree of *Juris Doctor*.
Other prominent schools are considering its adoption, Harvard
having already recommended such a change to its faculty and
students."[20] In a response the next day to the editor of *The*

Maroon, a student signed "Grad" questioned the legitimacy of the spelling of the degree:

> In your statement regarding the degree to be conferred on completion of the graduate law course you spell the title *Juris Doctor,* and employ the letters J.D. for the abbreviation. The Latin language never knew the letter J (j), but always used I (i), while in modern times the J is employed. Very correctly the department of Latin in the University of Chicago follows the style of ancient Rome and does not recognize a letter j in the Latin alphabet. I suggest, therefore, that *The Maroon* set the example for correct usage and print Iuris Doctor and I.D. Academic though the point may be, yet if it is correct to write I, and not J, it ought to be followed in actual practice.[21]

The editor's reply was appropriate: "Unfortunately for the 'Grad's' suggestion, President Harper favors the J.D."

Harper did indeed favor the J.D. degree, as did the law faculty, but for more serious reasons than that suggested by any differences of style in Latin spellings. The issue was a controversial one in legal education circles, and the Chicago position was a pioneering one. The traditional degree awarded by the American law schools continued to be the Bachelor of Laws (LL.B.). Because few lawyers had received a college degree prior to attending law school, their first earned degree was the law degree; thus the bachelor's designation was appropriate for that degree. Yet Harper's law school was to be a graduate law school with admission conditional on a college degree or, in exceptional cases, three years of college work. The case for higher admissions standards that would require a college background was strongly made by Harper. In announcing the complete plans of the Law School in October, Harper referred to the arguments in opposition to the requirement of a college degree for professional education. He alluded to the position taken by President Hadley of Yale, "who points out the undeniable fact that the higher standard shuts out many men otherwise well-qualified who cannot afford the expenditure of time and money involved in the longer preparation for their professional work." Not accepting this point of view, Harper maintained that the value of a liberal education prior to professional study would give "a higher meaning and interest to the practice of a learned profession."[22]

Harper also knew he was at the forefront of a movement and could proceed without the sanction of tradition. The Harvard Corporation had not yet acted upon the recommendation of the Harvard law faculty for the adoption of the new J.D. degree. Only Columbia and Stanford had approved the criterion of a college education for regular admission. Thus Harper announced proudly, "the University while conceding that law schools of the prevailing type were and would for a considerable time continue to be, a necessity, also realized the fact that its position and its resources gave it the opportunity, and made it its duty, to adopt the highest standard of legal education, and to establish its law school upon the foundation of academic work."[23] Ernst Freund made the same point less dramatically. "The J.D. degree introduced at Chicago," said Freund, "recognized the fact that law work done by college graduates was deserving of the same recognition as other graduate work."[24]

Harper had grand designs for the new Law School. He often expressed the hope that instruction would be provided for transfer students who wished to take the second and third years of the law course. Further, he wanted to provide special work for the connection of law with contemporary commercial life. In addition Harper proposed to provide instruction for students from other institutions who wanted to do special work in particular subjects, for practicing lawyers who wanted to conduct special study, and for teachers of law from other schools desiring to undertake advanced work "with professors of law of international reputation."[25] Thus his law school was to be more than a graduate school for college graduates, as it would provide opportunity for transfer students, special study at the post-J.D. level, continuing legal education, and special instruction for future law professors.

It is interesting to note that Freund's position in regard to the J.D. degree differed slightly from Harper's. Both men, as well as the other members of the law faculty, agreed that the study of law was a form of graduate study. But Freund did not support the view that the J.D. degree was comparable to the Ph.D. degree:

To some extent the appropriateness of the doctor's degree was also supported by the argument that the study of law on the basis of cases is a form of research; but in opposition to this contention it is insisted that it is not the mere use of original sources, but the independent discovery, collation, and sifting materials which in the graduate school constitutes the title to the doctorate, and that the only corresponding work in law schools—brief writing for moot courts or practice courses, or note writing for law reviews—is of too limited a scope to be reckoned as the equivalent of a thesis.[26]

Freund agreed with Harper and his colleagues on the requirement of an academic degree and the desirability of a liberal arts background. The position of the faculty on this issue was expressed by James Parker Hall. "There could be no question that a college education was the best preparation for legal study. Not only would a college education make the recipient a more capable person, but no one can doubt," Hall maintained, "that a college graduate is usually far better fitted seriously to study law and to get a good legal training in three years than is a boy of 18 or 19 from the high school." The J.D., Hall observed in response to an ABA recommendation for uniformity in law degrees, was simply, yet significantly, a new degree that separated the person who held a college degree from one who did not. "It is not," Hall said, "a degree heretofore used for postgraduate work, which it would be improper to pervert to some less dignified purpose."[27]

In a summary of the early days of the Law School, Hall stated additional reasons for the necessity of a collegiate background for law school. A person just out of high school could not comprehend either the basis of social experience upon which legal principles rested or the social problems which were pressing for solution. A college education provided a student with a background of major importance to his wider relation to the world outside the law:

In this country the capable lawyer is also the wise and
trusted adviser and man of affairs in many relations of life.
Such a role demands a flexibility and readiness of mind for
which no particular kind of study can be a specific preparation, but which is certainly better promoted by the varied
work and interests of college life than by any other known
course of training.[28]

The J.D., observed Hall, was a degree parallel with the J.U.D.
conferred in German universities, a degree which was not an
advanced or second degree in law. The German doctorate thus
represented the completion of the ordinary course of professional study, following the academic training obtained in the
gymnasium. The J.U.D., Hall noted, was not taken by people
whose interests were teaching or writing; it was the degree
taken by men studying to become lawyers and judges of the
German empire.

The Law Faculty Senate and the trustees concurred with the
arguments for the high standards of admission and the awarding of the J.D. to graduates who had earned a college degree.[29]
The first *Announcements* of the Law School stated: "The standards of requirements for admission constitute the school
practically a graduate school. In its requirements it equals
the best institutions in the country, and surpasses any
other law school in the West." Provisions were to be made for
admission following the prelegal curriculum, and credit would
be given to work done at other law schools. The adoption
of the high standards for admission were explained in the
Announcements in terms of the advantage of instructing a
homogeneous body of students who had received the training
deemed "best calculated to develop intellectual power."[30] Prospective students were informed that they might save one
year by combining the final year of college and the first year of
Law School.

The second *Announcements* described in more detail the
reasons for the Law School's demanding admissions standards,
noting that the organization of the school "presented the problem of the proper adjustment between academic and professional work." The statement pointed out that only one law
school in the Middle West required more than completion of a

high school course for admission, that institution being Ohio State, which required two years of preliminary college work. Nationally, Chicago's position was immediately established as representing the highest admissions standards in legal education. The *Announcements* stated that "the two foremost law schools in the country had just raised, or were about to raise, the standard of admission to the requirement of a college degree."[31] Beale had brought many ideas with him from Cambridge and was aware that the Harvard law faculty in 1902 had recommended to the Harvard Corporation that the J.D. degree be adopted. But Harvard did not move quickly on the recommendation.[32]

Not only was there disagreement at Harvard over the proper nomenclature for the first earned degree, but when the Law School opened at Chicago confusion occurred that went beyond the "J.D./I.D." question posed by the pedantic graduate student. Henry P. Chandler, later a graduate of the Law School, but then serving as secretary to the university's President Judson, wrote to Hall, asking: "Mr. Judson notes that in our alumni directory the degree of J.D. is spelled out 'Doctor of Jurisprudence'. He thinks that this is wrong and that the proper English translation of Juris Doctor is Doctor of Law. Can you advise us?"[33] Mr. Judson's case was firmly established by Hall's response. "The proper English translation of Juris Doctor is Doctor of Law," Hall declared. *."Jus* means, literally, the science of rights, unwritten law, as distinguished from *lex*, which means written law. The phrase 'Doctor of Jurisprudence' we hold in just abhorrence."[34]

The second *Announcements* of the Law School stipulated the university's position on the awarding of the LL.B. degree. Late in the summer of 1902 the law faculty approved the establishment of the LL.B. degree "upon the completion of [the regular] curriculum to special students . . . those qualified to enter the Junior College."[35] Hall described the rationale of the degree by noting that there were a large number of students throughout the Middle West with promising ability, many of them principals and superintendents, who had not completed a college course. These students would be admitted to the professional program if they were over twenty-one years of age and had completed a four-year high school course. Their admission was conditional upon them maintaining a grade average 10 percent higher than that required for passing. Thus by demanding a "specially high quality of work from this class of students, a check will be placed upon the indiscriminate admission of special students, and the character of the school as a graduate school will be maintained."[36]

Recruiting Students for a National Law School

Having determined that the standards for admission were to be among the highest existing in legal education, the faculty then turned to the task of student recruitment. At the first faculty meeting, Beale and Freund were appointed to be in charge of publicity. Following the formal approval by the trustees of the plans of organization of the new school, flyers and circulars of information were sent to colleges across the country, announcements were put in various university journals and publications, and other forms of advertising were prepared, including notices in newspapers. The task of admitting students was assigned to Freund and Lee.

The first *Announcements* of the Law School made it clear that, contrary to existing practices, students were expected to give their whole time to the study of law. Furthermore, students would not be encouraged to work in law offices during the academic year. In acknowledgment that the traditional law office education had some value, it was stated that special provision would be made for instruction in the drafting of documents and in court practice. Between quarters students could attend court sessions for observation of the trial of cases. But the study of law at Chicago would demand the entire time of the student.

Because of the high standards, as well as the brief period available for creating the school, Harper had not envisaged a large number of students the first year. In December 1902, two months after classes had begun, he spoke about the new school at convocation. "It is somewhat difficult for me to describe the feeling of satisfaction which, I think, exists throughout the University in view of the fact that the Law School is at last actually organized and its work in process of accomplishment," Harper began. Observing that the requirements for admission exceeded those of any school west of New York, he noted that "it was hardly to be expected that a large body of students would come together during the first Quarter." The quality of the students, who numbered nearly eighty, was also a source of great satisfaction to Harper: "The general character of the students and their intellectual ability have been the subject of most favorable comment on the part of all who have come into contact with them. Their devotion to the work of their particular school and the interest taken by them in the University at large deserves special mention."[37]

The official *Register* of the university for 1902–3 indicated that seventy-six men and two women were enrolled in the professional program and an additional twenty in the preprofessional program. Thirty-nine were first-year professional students, twelve were enrolled in the second-year program, and eight in the third-year program. Forty students in the professional program came from the University of Chicago. The rest of the first class of students came from schools that included Berkeley, Harvard, Illinois, Missouri, Montana State, Stanford, Toronto, and Wheaton. The students were likewise widely distributed in their geographic origins. In the first year thirteen states and Canada were represented. The states with the largest number of students were Illinois (thirty-two, eight of whom were from outside Chicago), Indiana (five), Kansas (five), Iowa (four), and California, Kentucky, and Wisconsin with two students each.[38]

The fact that Chicago was firmly established as a national law school was made further evident by the figures for the next year. The number of students in the professional program had increased from seventy-eight to one hundred twenty-six. Forty-nine schools were represented as opposed to sixteen from the year before, and only 33 percent of the students had come from the University of Chicago as opposed to 50 percent in 1902. The geographical distribution of students had likewise increased in diversity. The states with more than one student represented in 1903 were Illinois (fifty-two, with eighteen from outside of Chicago), Iowa (nineteen), Kansas and Wisconsin (six each), Indiana (five), Kentucky (four), Texas (three), and Michigan, Missouri, Ohio, Mississippi, and Minnesota (two each). Canada had three students in residence. Thus the number of states represented had more than doubled, from thirteen to twenty-seven.[39]

Students came to Chicago for many reasons, despite the fact that the school had the reputation for being "tough and all business."[40] One early alumnus, Edward J. Clark, recalls that his decision was made upon the recommendation of his Latin teacher, who used texts by Harper.[41] Another, Albrecht R. C. Kipp, notes that Laird Bell and Edgar Noble Durfee, both Harvard College graduates, persuaded him to enroll, "pointing out rightly the professors were Harvard men, the classes were smaller and the competition tougher."[42]

It is not known whether the proposed unofficial loan of Harvard students to Chicago for several terms of study actually happened. The *Register* notes one student from Harvard the first year and three from Harvard the second. Conceivably these students may have been at Chicago as a result of the proposal. However, at least one of them, Robert Hunt, was on loan from Harvard, although the circumstances surrounding his presence were less than desirable as a regular feature for exchange between the two cooperating institutions. Hunt had experienced serious academic problems at Harvard and had been in trouble outside the classroom, much to the unhappiness of his well-to-do father, who exerted great pressure on Eliot to get him through Harvard. In his first report to Eliot on the new school Beale began with an evaluation of the work on Hunt: "First, as to Hunt, I have just written his father a favorable account of his work. I know very little of his life outside the classes though I have some reason to believe he is doing well. In class," Beale continued, "I have found him always prepared, and better still I almost always find him alive to the question under discussion, interested and intelligent. I hope it will be just what he needed to be in a small class and constantly under the eye of the teacher."[43]

It is clear that students from other law schools transferred to Chicago. In a report in the spring of 1903 Harper spoke of transfer students as well as of the presence at the school of nondegree candidates who were practicing lawyers. One reason these students were attracted, Harper suggested, was that "the presence of lectures of so strong a body of men seems already to have been appreciated by those who desire to use the summer months in the prosecution of their law studies."[44]

Perhaps the most significant departure from existing traditions in legal education was the admission of women into the Law School. The first class had two women, including Sophonisba Preston Breckenridge, who became a guiding force in the establishment of the university's school of Social Service Administration and a pioneer in the field of social services and welfare agencies. Women were not eligible for admission to Yale until 1918, to Columbia Law School until 1927, and to Harvard until 1950. The earliest record of a woman law graduate had been in 1872 from Michigan. In 1899 a woman was granted admission to Harvard Law School, but the action was rescinded several months later. For the next two years the Cambridge Law School for women law students was conducted by Harvard professors, but that experiment was discontinued.[45]

The law schools were decidedly a man's world, reflecting the opinion of the bar that the practice of law was a male jurisdiction. In 1872 the issue of women at the bar was first raised at Harvard and Yale. Miss Helen M. Sawyer applied for admission at Harvard. Since no statute existed for this situation, it was referred to the Harvard Corporation, which, after two full discussions, rejected her application. Harvard did not graduate its first alumna until 1957.

Stumped by the same novel issue, Yale too turned to the Yale Corporation, which decided against female law students. At least one mitigating factor in the case against women in law was reflected in the letter to Yale officials from George C. Still: "Are you far advanced enough to admit young women to your school? In theory I am in favor of their studying & practising law, provided they are *ugly*, but I should fear a handsome woman before a jury."[46] In 1885 a woman applicant at Yale took an assertive approach. Showing up at registration, Alice Rufie Jordan, who had received a B.S. from the University of Michigan and was a member of the Michigan bar, demanded admission, citing the fact that the catalogue did not bar women. Dean Francis Wayland allowed her to enroll, but President Noah Porter and the Yale Corporation had other reactions. After discussion, the corporation ruled she could not be listed as an official student but did not forbid her to take classes. Undaunted, Miss Jordan completed her work and received her LL.B. in 1886. The Corporation reacted by directing the following statement be placed in future catalogues of the college: "It is to be understood that the courses of instruction are open to persons of the male sex only, except where both sexes are specifically included."[47] This warning statement appeared in the university catalogue until 1918–19, although it was never included in the Law School Bulletin.[48]

The Harvard position on women in law school was amplified in the minutes of a law faculty meeting which occurred some time in 1896 or 1897. The question before the faculty concerned the desirability of allowing graduate students at Radcliffe to register in selective Law School courses. Christopher Columbus Langdell "declines to express an opinion—the question not being [formally] before us." The others present agreed in principle to the presence of the Radcliffe students, but their reservations are revealing. Dean Ames commented that he would support the idea "but personally would regret it." Thayer remarked that he "personally does want them." Gray concurred, "but does not want them to come and does not advise." Smith conceded that he thought "*some* women would make good lawyers." Wambaugh allowed that he did "not advise women to study law and prefers not to have women in the school." Finally, Beale noted that this move would require "special instruction in first-year courses."[49]

Beatrice Doerschuk's 1915 survey, *Women in The Law*, found that the "net proportion of women admitted to the bar and applying their legal training is probably less than half of those who attend law school." Her survey indicated that the five law schools at that time with the largest number of women graduates were Northwestern (forty), Michigan (twenty-nine), Iowa (twenty-five), Minnesota (twenty), and Chicago (seventeen). Thus the trend had been decidedly a midwestern phenomenon among larger law schools, with the exception of Chicago, which had a relatively small student body. In 1915 the seven schools with the largest enrollment of women were Chicago (twelve), Berkeley (six), University of Washington (six), Northwestern (four), Cornell (four), University of Pennsylvania (four), and Wisconsin (four).[50]

Harper's view on coeducation had been frequently voiced.

The East, according to Harper, was at least fifty years behind the West. One reason for this fact, suggested Harper, was economic necessity. "How could provision be made in the western states for separate colleges for women when there were so few such colleges for men?" But with so many students in his day interested in higher education, Harper was persuaded that the coeducational trend would continue. With his characteristic flourish, Harper predicted: "The Spirit which opens the doors of educational institutions to women as well as to men is, one may safely say, splendidly modern and higher than the older spirit of the monastery or the convent. It is surely more American." The question for Harper was not whether there should be coeducation but how it could be accomplished. Thus he concluded, "coeducation demands for its acceptance as a principle, association of men and women in educational work, on absolutely equal terms, and under the same general management. . . . there is not only ample room, but a stern demand, for liberty of action as well as of thought, in those things which pertain to the further development of this policy."[51]

Marion Talbot, the dean of women at the university, provided additional insight for the question of women on the Midway. In 1892, when the university first conducted classes, the proportion of women enrolled was 24 percent. By 1901, on the eve of the opening of the Law School, the percentage, which had risen steadily during the past decade, was 52. In her autobiography, *More than Lore*, Dean Talbot observed that in 1898–99, fifty men and fifty-two women received honorable mention, honor scholarships, and honors in the departments. "An explanation of this situation is hinted at," Talbot wryly observed, "in the remark of a bumptious young man student who was serving as a messenger in one of the administration offices: 'No man can lower himself by competing with girls in the classroom.' " The increasing proportion of women undergraduates was an alarming situation, according to Talbot, who urged Harper to make the university more attractive to men. "Within three or four years the following means of serving men were inaugurated: Bartlett Gymnasium, Reynolds Club, Hutchinson Commons, Hitchcock Hall, and the Law School."[52]

Whether the law faculty was aware of their role in this "conspiracy" to meet the problem posed by the increasing number

of women on campus is unclear. There is no evidence, however,
that the law faculty ever considered excluding women from
the Law School. One alumna of the Law School, Eileen Markely
Znaniecki, recalled that James Parker Hall did question her
about her motivations as a prospective woman lawyer. He also
questioned her desire to do legal-aid work. Mrs. Znaniecki had
been rejected at Columbia despite the fact that her father had
received his law degree there, and she had received her master's
degree from Columbia. "Dean Hall, however, said that a young
lady who had taken some courses had scandalized the University by sitting out on the lawn surrounded by a circle of ador-
ing law students. When I assured him that my only interest
was in learning enough law to help the poor, he was reassured.
However, he tried to discourage my interest in Legal Aid,
saying the matters were too small to be important and that
the lawyers were apt to be below University of Chicago
standards."[53]

Writing for the university's annual yearbook, _The Cap and
Gown_, a student pondered the symbolic significance of the Law
School's new home:

> Was the location of the Law Building a chance, or is it
> significant that, standing as it does between the halls of men
> on one side and the halls of women on the other, it seems
> to hold its four spires heavenward in a mute plea for justice,
> equality, and now segregation? Does the small entrance on
> the east stand as an invitation for more Portias to become
> Balthasars or is it merely to afford an avenue of escape for
> the weary minds of the prospective juris doctor's to soothing
> influence? Only the faculty know, and only the future will
> reveal.[54]

The annual _Cap and Gown_ provides interesting further information concerning the students who were attracted to the
new Law School.[55] Most had had extensive extracurricular activities as undergraduates. Many continued these activities
after arriving on the Midway, an indication that the law students mixed freely in university activities. Award winners in
public speaking and oratory contests were common. One early
law student, Henry Porter Chandler, served as advisor to the
college debate team. Editors of college yearbooks and news-

papers, presidents and officers of student government, debating champions, fraternity officers, and officers in campus political organizations were frequently furnished by the Law School. Of particular note were the many men who had participated in intercollegiate athletics. The law students quickly strengthened the university's football efforts. The *Maroon* reported that "we have a football team and the Laws 'joined in.' Then they persuaded some football men to become laws, and brought back, as grads, other active men." Indeed the Laws, as the law students were immediately called within the university community, created their own football yell:

Rah! rah! U rah! Who are we?
Law School! Law School! U of C![56]

In both debate and athletics the Laws became major participants. Law students also became active in the governance of the Reynolds Club, which had been designed to resemble a city club and to create a clubhouse for men in order "to provide a four-square education, in the liberal arts, in science, in gymnastics, and in 'the manners that make men.' "[57] Harper observed the close relation between the Law School and the rest of the university soon after the school opened:

The Law School of the University of Chicago is not an institution which has a merely nominal connection with the University, and is separated either by local arrangements or in spirit from the University. Its students are breathing the University atmosphere, and are distracted by vain efforts to combine the practical and the theoretical.[58]

Law clubs were quickly established at Chicago. Beale had emphasized to Harper the importance of these organizations for the spirit of the school as well as for their educational value through discussion of legal questions. Two members of each club prepared opposite sides of a disputed point in law and argued the point before the club. Two men served as a chief justice and a clerk. At the close of the argument, the club members would render a decision. This Harvard idea was to be brought to Chicago for use by first-year students only. Advanced students would argue before moot courts. The first law club, a feature which had been advertised in the advance pro-

motion of the new school, was organized early in 1902. Known
as the Joseph Beale, Jr., Law Club, its first session open to the
university at large was held on November 18 and carefully
reported in *The Maroon*. In an initiative of a different nature,
eight students organized a social club, the Woolsack Society,
which was the forerunner of the first law fraternity on campus,
Phi Delta Phi. The Stephen A. Douglas chapter of Phi Delta Phi
was not officially chartered until April 14, 1903; it was sponsored by Beale, Mechem, Freund, Mack, Whittier, Hall, and
Kremer. One month later the Chicago chapter of Delta Chi,
another law fraternity, was established.[59]

Both Harper and Beale had hoped to establish a law review
at Chicago. As such a publication was one of Harvard's most
distinctive traditions, Beale wanted the journal to be established quickly. The value of law reviews was widely acknowledged following the first issue of Harvard's review, which
appeared in 1887. "The *Law Review* provides some very useful
legal commentary," Erwin Griswold maintained decades later.
"It tends to be too tightly written for easy reading, and to bury
itself in footnotes designed to show that students have been
diligent and have not overlooked any possible relevant materials. But the achievement is a remarkable one, that in a
learned profession the basic periodical commentaries are written and edited by students."[60] It is safe to assume that one of
Harper's motivations for establishing a law review involved
his constant advocacy of scholarly journals that would be published by the university and that would further its prestige and
usefulness.

But a law review at Chicago would not materialize until the
early 1930s. Some years after the founding of the school, Hall,
in a letter recommending a new law journal to be jointly sponsored with the University of Illinois and Northwestern, observed that there were several reasons why Chicago had not
published a law journal, "despite its obvious advantages."
First, Hall recalled, "during the early years of the School our
Faculty was small and the work incidental to organizing the
School, creating good traditions of work among the students,
and mastering our curriculum, left no time for such an enterprise." The major reason cited by Hall, however, was the financial one. The cost of the many journals encouraged by Harper

was a constant concern to Rockefeller and his associates. "Up to the time of the war," Hall continued, "the number of our alumni was too small to support such a journal, and we did not feel like asking the University to add to its already heavy burden of permanently subsidizing journals." The final reason posed by Hall was the opinion of the law faculty that there was no public need for another law review of "the ordinary sort, though it would no doubt be of some benefit to our Faculty and students."[61]

Another policy established by the law faculty early in the organizational days concerned scholarships. At their first meeting they voted to ask the trustees for six tuition scholarships. Recipients were to work two and one-half hours daily as library helpers in compensation for the scholarships. The next year the faculty increased their request to ten scholarships. The use of scholarship recipients to staff the library was not a satisfactory policy to at least one member of the faculty. Writing to Harper, Mack acknowledged the necessity but noted "it is at times a hardship on men ambitious to cover as much work as possible during their course—countless many men would prefer to borrow the amount of this tuition rather than sacrifice the time that the University asks of its beneficiaries. This is particularly true of professional students."[62] To remedy this situation, Mack established a loan fund, expressing the hope it would attract similar gifts to the Law School as well as to other departments.

As was evident by his policy in other parts of the university, Harper believed that scholarship money would be necessary to attract the best students to Chicago. Moreover, scholarships would enhance the reputation of the university. Writing to Hall during the second year of the school's existence, Harper suggested that "you pick out twenty colleges not included in the number of those that have a student representative in our Law School at present, and . . . write to the President of each of these colleges that a scholarship in the Law School for one year can be arranged for a graduate of the college, to be named by the faculty. As we are manned to-day we can easily care for these twenty extra students and it would kindle a new interest in twenty new centers."[63]

Harper had initially hoped that the Law School would be

self-supporting. The tuition fee was set at $50 a quarter and would cover the regular work, that is, three majors or their equivalent. Students from the college or the Graduate School of Arts, Literature, and Science would be encouraged to enroll and were to pay a special fee of $5 for each major course. The *Announcements* contained an estimate of the annual expenses for thirty-six weeks for a law student residing within the quadrangles. Including tuition, room and board, laundry, textbooks, and stationery, prospective students were told to anticipate an average expense of $436.

The first report from the university's counsel and business manager, Wallace Heckman, to the trustees of receipts and expenditures for the Law School indicated that Harper's hopes for a self-sustaining law school were not being fulfilled. Receipts totaled $10,311 and expenditures came to $21,134, with instruction counting for $18,491 of the total expense. The funds for the purchase of the law library had been allocated previously from gift funds from Rockefeller. Nor was the situation to improve the second year, despite the increased number of students: receipts rose to $15,603 but the expenditures increased to $34,054 as the instructional costs rose to $29,786. Of the six other reports on departmental expenses, three reported deficits substantially larger than the Law School's: the Morgan Park Academy, the School of Education, and Printing and Publishing. Only one department showed a surplus, the Divinity School, whose total expenditures were $69,226, leaving a $61.72 surplus. The University Extension and the University College showed lesser deficits.[64]

It is interesting that the department showing the highest cost per student in the 1902 report was the Law School. By the third year, as attendance in the school increased, the expenditures stabilized and the Law School had the lowest cost per student and Harper's earlier predictions seemed closer to realization.[65] By 1909 the number of law students had risen to 300 from the initial 78 and Harper's hopes had yet to be vindicated. In fact receipts came to $34,000 and expenditures had reached $54,000. The difference was met by income from the Rockefeller Endowment Fund for the Faculties of Arts, Literature, and Science.[66] Nevertheless, it is important to observe that Harper was correct in assuring the trustees that the cost of establishing and conducting the Law School was considerably less than for other graduate departments and professional schools.

A Home for Harper's Law School

Early in 1902, as the momentum for the approval of the proposed Law School increased, different opinions concerning the location of the school were voiced. Initially the University Senate recommended that the school be housed with the School of Education.[67] Beale, in his negotiations with Harper in late winter, expressed grave concern about whether the school should be opened at all without a building of its own. But Harper pushed ahead, not only for temporary quarters, but for a permanent home for the school. The prospect of securing funds for the new building was not promising even though Harper had been for some time waging a strenuous campaign for financial support from the Chicago community. Never one to be daunted, especially in financial matters, Harper turned again to Rockefeller, who had already consented to support the law library. At a meeting of the trustees on April 15, 1902, the day on which the law faculty met for the first time, the following recommendation was submitted:

> That Mr. Rockefeller be requested to guarantee $200,000 for the erection of a building for the Law School, the Board of Trustees agreeing to make every effort to secure this sum elsewhere, and relieve him from the payment of the money.[68]

The request was subsequently made by Harper and the trustees. The founder's response, as conveyed by John D. Rockefeller, Jr., was read to the board at their May 1 meeting. In addition to agreeing to the request, Rockefeller asked that accommodations be such that a thousand law students could be handled. The implication was financial, as law schools the size of Harvard's and Michigan's brought in substantial revenues for their parent institutions. Rockefeller made two additional provisions. First, "that the fact of this guarantee shall be kept absolutely within the Board of Trustees and that every effort should be made to secure a large part, and if possible the whole, of the $200,000 from other sources." Moreover, until the Law School student body reached a thousand, sections of the new building were to be used to relieve the present crowded condition of the History Department.[69] The trustees accepted these provisions and then proceeded to approve the selection of the Boston architectural firm of Shepley, Rutan and Coolidge to draw up plans. The architect was to be Frederick Olmsted.

At least the last condition of the founder was met; the libraries of history, political economy, philosophy, and anthropology used stack space in the Law School building for many years and professors in these departments were accommodated with offices there. There is no indication, however, that Harper or the trustees ever tried to obtain funds to repay the Rockefeller commitment. A later exchange between Harold Swift and John D. Rockefeller, Jr., concerning the possibility of naming the Law School building in memory of the father in exchange for a contribution from the Rockefeller family reveals that any moral commitment to replace the funds had been canceled. The original documents which had been reviewed by Swift indicated "this was probably amply covered in conversation at the time."[70] Casting aside the suggestion concerning the memorial to his father, Rockefeller's response indicated agreement concerning the cancellation of financial obligations.[71] The $10 million gift made by the senior Rockefeller on December 1, 1910, intended as his "final gift," had released the university from any amounts due the family.

The size of the building, hence its ability to accommodate the number of students stipulated by Rockefeller, did not meet the conditions of his gift. The Library Commission recommended to the trustees that the Law School building be located east of and across the roadway from Haskell Museum.[72] Not all members of the university community agreed. A report of the Committee on the Placing of Buildings for Instruction and Research, appointed by the University Senate, submitted an opinion that professional studies did not belong on the central campus. With "remarkable unanimity," the members of the committee emphasized the threat of congestion on the Midway. According to the committee, the core of the university from the beginning had encompassed nonprofessional study, and many faculty wished to keep it that way. "The Committee is of the strong opinion that this campus should be used, so far as existing obligations permit, only for non-professional study, i.e., for what must always remain the nucleus, as it was [from] the beginning of the University." Therefore, the committee urged that "no law or other professional schools be established on the present campus."[73]

The argument submitted by the committee, which had viewed an architectural plan of the campus, was twofold. First, was "primarily the consideration of fitness." But second, the committee felt that as much space as possible ought to be saved on campus. Although the basis for this position was not clear, the committee felt that the "School of Law, like the School of Education, and technological and other schools that may hereafter be established ought to be conspicuously visible as differentiable parts of the University, from the Midway drive." A notation appeared in pencil on top of the report, indicating that the recommendations that had been made to the senate by the committee had been tabled, "to be called up at the President's discretion."[74] These recommendations were, of course, unacceptable to Harper because they ran contrary to his strongly held opinion on the organic nature of the university. The same day that the senate tabled the motion, the University Council approved the motion to ask the library to give up the catalogue room assigned it in the Press building for a smaller one and, by this move, as well as other adjustments, to find room in the Press building for temporary quarters for the Law School.[75]

The plans for the new building continued, and it was soon learned that the projected cost would be about $330,000. On October 7 The Maroon observed that Beale, Harper, and a "Mr. Olmsted," a landscape architect from the Boston firm commissioned to plan the building, had met and talked over the plans that would "bring both landscape and building designs into harmony." The building was to be three stories high, 175 feet long, and 80 feet wide, built of Bedford stone in the English Gothic style of architecture.[76] Because of the projected cost the trustees agreed at their November 10 meeting that the rear addition to the building should be left off, thus reducing the cost to $250,000. As the building was to be shared with other departments, the number of law students who could be accommodated was reduced.[77]

But until the building was finished, the students and faculty would have to live with the inconveniences of temporary quarters, reassured by the opinion of Harper that it could be "confidently asserted that upon the completion of the building, no law school will possess physical advantages superior to those of the Law School of this University."[78] In the temporary quarters, space for one large lecture room was assigned on the second floor, and the larger part of the third floor was devoted to a reading room, stack room, and a small lecture room. The reading room was ready for occupancy only a few hours before the school actually opened on October 1. Hall recalled that the "tables had not come, and in their stead were long boards covered with heavy paper and stretched across saw-horses, upon which were prepared the first lessons in the new School." Hall also recalled a visit he and Harper made to the prospective quarters two days before the school opened. Harper, seeing the rooms stacked high with debris, sent a vigorous message to the superintendent of buildings and grounds: "There are to be lectures here in 48 hours and it will take longer than that to clean up these rooms."[79]

But the school did open on October 1, 1902, despite the confusion and the many problems resulting from the short time available for performing a myriad of tasks. Beale had wanted Justice Oliver Wendell Holmes to give an inaugural oration. Harper did not agree, largely because of the grand design he had in mind that would bring President Theodore Roosevelt to the Midway to lay the cornerstone for the law building—an event which would prove to be one of the most elaborate in the early history of the university. But that celebration would mark another chapter in the early days of Harper's experiment in legal education.[80] *The Maroon* heralded the opening day with the headline: "New Law School a Success." An editorial stated that the "Law School opened its doors for the first time today in its spacious temporary home in the Press building with every indication that it will be a pronounced success."[81]

Off to an immediate start, the Law School was the only department within the university that held classes on the first day. Thus, the *Maroon* continued, " 'Laws' from Wisconsin, Harvard, Northwestern, and Stanford are adding their names to the registration rolls and swelling the number." An editorial the next day warmly welcomed the new members of the university community:

> . . . the "Laws" are today taking their place as a part of the University. The character and aims of the men of this new department and the circumstances under which they come to us make them truly deserving of the hearty welcome extended to them by faculty and students. The majority of the men who yesterday enrolled in the Law School come to Chicago from other colleges and universities. They bring with them a wealth of experience and knowledge of things essentially collegiate.[82]

Freund and Beale, who as Dean had to register each student personally, were quoted: "It is now assured that the attendance will be all that could be expected and, to say the least, decidedly gratifying."[83] Soon after, Harper proudly acknowledged the events preceding and surrounding the opening of the school. "It is an organic part of the University. It makes valuable contribution to the University life and at the same time it imbibes the spirit and the purpose of that life." William Rainey Harper's dream had become a reality. Although the Law School had had a long gestation, the actual birth had happened quickly, in the fashion that characterized the building of Harper's great university. Harper concluded his report to the university community, prophesizing as he was always wont to do about future greatness, "if the future of the school may be measured by the success thus far achieved, there is ground for sincere satisfaction."[84]

Notes

Notes to Chapter One

1. Woodrow Wilson, "Legal Education of Undergraduates," *Proceedings of the 1894 Annual Meeting of the American Bar Association* (1894), pp. 439–40. See Richard Hofstadter, *The Age of Reform* (New York: Random House, 1955), pp. 174–214. For an interesting analysis of the reform movements as they relate to the legal profession, see Jerold A. Auerbach, *Unequal Justice: Lawyers and Social Change in Modern America* (New York: Oxford University Press, 1976), pp. 18–20.

2. See Laurence Edmund Sommers, "Lawyers and Progressive Reform: A Study of Attitudes in Illinois 1890–1920" (Ph.D. diss., Northwestern University, 1967), pp. 77–81. See also David F. Burg, *Chicago's White City of 1893* (Lexington: University Press of Kentucky, 1976); Hubert Howe Bancroft, *The Book of the Fair: An Historical and Descriptive Presentation of the World's Science, Art, and Industry, as Viewed through the Columbian Exposition at Chicago in 1893* (New York: Bounty Books, 1894); and Charles Carroll Bonney, *World's Congress Addresses* (Chicago: Open Court Publishing Company, 1900).

3. The Bradwell quotation is from Herman Kogan's *The First Century: The Chicago Bar Association, 1874–1974* (Chicago: Rand McNally, 1974), p. 15.

4. Ibid., pp. 25–33.

5. Quoted in ibid., p. 30.

6. Ibid., pp. 42–43. The 1876 study by the grievance committee noted that, since its origin, the organization had taken in $8,625 in fees and dues and $1,500 for three annual dinners. "For all of this —what do we have to show? A little furniture, rarely used; a few legal periodicals, never read; one divorce lawyer disbarred and pursuing his nefarious traffic with more brazen impunity than before; three dinners, eaten in the past, and the absolute proprietorship of a janitor *in praesenti* and *in futuro*." See George Martin, *Causes and Conflicts—The Centennial History of the Association of the Bar of the City of New York, 1870–1970* (Boston: Houghton Mifflin, 1970).

7. Quoted in Kogan, *Chicago Bar*, p. 63.

8. Ibid., pp. 63–77.

9. Sommers, "Lawyers and Progressive Reform," p. 79. Sommers argues that a liberal minority of prominent lawyers led the bar in supporting middle-class reforms and concludes that the reform efforts diminished as the organized bar became stronger in the early twentieth century.

10. Until 1941 no admission criteria existed. A perfunctory examination in open court was the only requirement. In 1887 the Chicago Bar Association's Committee on Legal Education declared that the existing requirements were "wholly inadequate . . . many incompetent persons, not learned in law, are licensed as attorneys and counselors and thereby the profession and the public are alike injured" (in Kogan, *Chicago Bar*, p. 83). The committee asked the state supreme court to appoint a board of examiners and suggested that each applicant be a graduate of an established law school, or have served as an apprentice for three years, or a combination of both. In 1889 the committee pushed again for the same proposal, noting the increased role law schools might play. But the response was again negative.

11. Quoted in Kogan, *Chicago Bar*, p. 84. The Chicago College of Law, a proprietary school later known as Chicago Kent College of Law, began in 1877 in the chambers of Judge Joseph Bailey of Freeport, who taught his clerks there. As interest grew, classes were moved to his courtroom and conducted in his off hours under the name of the Chicago Evening College of Law. The school is now affiliated with the Illinois Institute of Technology.

12. Quoted in ibid., p. 85.

13. Ibid., p. 22.

14. For the history of the old university, see C. H. Koenitzer, "History of the First University of Chicago, 1856–1886" (Chicago: n.p., 1927 or 1928); Arthur A. Azlein, "The Old University of Chicago" (a D.B. paper, University of Chicago, 1941); James A. Rahl and Kurt Schwerin, *Northwestern University School of Law: A Short History* (Chicago: n.p., 1960), pp. 5–12; Thomas Wakefield Goodspeed, *A History of The University of Chicago* (Chicago: University of Chicago Press, 1916), pp. 12–20; and Richard J. Storr, *Harper's University: The Beginnings* (Chicago: University of Chicago Press, 1966), pp. 3–6.

15. Thomas M. Hoyne, Jr. "Reminiscences of Thomas M. Hoyne," *The [Northwestern] Alumni Journal* 16 (1916): 29.

16. Koenitzer, "History of the First University," p. 28.

17. Northwestern University Board of Trustees, Trustee Minutes: June 21, 1854, p. 49; June 6 and 7, 1857, pp. 95–96, 100; June 28, 1858, p. 137; July 9, 1858, p. 140; March 5, 1859, p. 151; April 4, 1859, p. 159; and June 24, 1875, pp. 115–16.

18. *Chicago Daily News,* June 28, p. 474, and August 30, 1870, pp. 474, 546.

19. Azlein, "Old University," p. 28. The old university was referred to as both "Chicago University" and "University of Chicago" throughout its twenty-nine-year history.

20. James E. Babb, "Union College of Law," *The Green Bag* 1 (1889): 330–38.

21. Frank H. Childs in a letter to Dr. D. M. Somerville, April 5, 1939, in Rahl and Schwerin, *Northwestern,* p. 11.

22. Ibid.

23. Babb, "Union College," p. 338.

24. Rahl and Schwerin, *Northwestern,* pp. 6–7, 11–12.

25. *The University Cases* (Chicago: Beach, Barnard & Co., 1884).

26. *Chicago Daily News,* January 9, 1885.

27. *Standard,* January 15, 1885.

28. Goodspeed, *University of Chicago,* p. 19.

29. Sheldon Tefft, "The Law School at the University of Chicago," *Oxonian* 50 (1963): 14.

30. Rahl and Schwerin, *Northwestern,* pp. 12–18.

31. William Rainey Harper, *The Trend in Higher Education* (Chicago: University of Chicago Press, 1905), p. 31.

32. Ibid., pp. 32, 35.

33. Ibid., pp. vii–viii.

34. Ibid., p. 6.

35. Ibid., p. 101.

36. Ibid., pp. 28–29.

37. William Rainey Harper, quoted in Storr, *Harper's University,* p. 24.

38. Ibid., p. 47.

39. Harper to Goodspeed, November 28, 1888, Special Collections, Regenstein Library, University of Chicago (this source hereafter cited as Regenstein).

40. William Rainey Harper, "Quarterly Statement of the President," *Quarterly Calendar* 2 (August, 1893): 9.

41. For a discussion of the initial plan see Storr, *Harper's University,* pp. 60–64.

42. *Official Bulletin No. 1* (1891), pp. 15–16.

43. Robert Herrick. "The Aims of the University," *Scribner's Magazine* 18 (1895): 413.

44. *Official Bulletin No. 1,* pp. 7–8.

45. Joseph H. Beale, Jr., "The Place of Professional Education in the Universities," *University Record* 9 (1905): 43.

46. William Rainey Harper, "The Urban University," reprinted in *Trend in Higher Education,* pp. 459, 460.

47. "Report of the Conference between Messrs. F. T. Gates,

T. W. Goodspeed, and H. A. Rust, with reference to The University
of Chicago," February 10, 1897, p. 8, Regenstein.

48. See Storr, *Harper's University*, pp. 258–80.

49. Ibid., p. 244.

50. "Report of the Conference," pp. 10–11.

51. E. L. Corthell to Harper, October 25, 1893, Regenstein.

52. See Storr, *Harper's University*, pp. 133–35; 285–87.

53. Ibid., pp. 135–41.

54. John Dewey, "Pedagogy as a University Discipline," *Record*
1 (1896): 354.

55. See Storr, *Harper's University*, pp. 339–41.

56. Thomas Wakefield Goodspeed, *William Rainey Harper* (Chicago: University of Chicago Press, 1928), p. 191.

57. William Rainey Harper, *Trend in Higher Education*, p. 368.

58. George H. Hopkins to Harper, March 13, 1893, Regenstein.
For a discussion of the Rush negotiations, see Ernest E. Irons, *The
Story of Rush Medical College* (Chicago: n.p., 1953), pp. 32–38. See
also Ilza Veith and Franklin C. McLean, *The University of Chicago
Clinics and Clinical Departments, 1927–1952* (Chicago: n.p., 1952),
pp. 1–6.

59. Gates to Goodspeed, January 12, 1893, Regenstein.

60. William Rainey Harper, "Quarterly Statement," *Record* 2
(1898): 322.

61. As Storr suggests, Rockefeller's reluctance is a puzzling issue, for Rockefeller was interested in medical education as is evident from his founding of the Rockefeller Institute for Medical Research in 1901. See Storr, *Harper's University*, pp. 286–91.

Notes to Chapter Two

1. William Rainey Harper, *The University of Chicago, The First
Annual Report* (1892).

2. Ibid.

3. William Rainey Harper, "Quarterly Statement of the President," *Quarterly Calendar* 2 (1893): 9.

4. Harper to Henry L. Morehouse, November 11, 1890, Regenstein.

5. William Rainey Harper, newspaper interview, quoted in the
University Weekly, October 26, 1893, p. 6.

6. Thomas J. Lawrence, "Memorial on the Creation of a Law
School in the University of Chicago," January 2, 1893, Regenstein.

7. Biographical information on Lawrence is in the *Annual Register, July 1, 1893–July, 1894* (Chicago: University of Chicago Press,
1894), p. 11.

8. Lawrence, "Memorial." In his memo Lawrence outlined in
detail a proposed course for the university extension on "The
Rulers and Makers of England," based on the principle that "the

history of the U.S. is only a continuation under happier conditions of the History of England."

9. For discussions of Harper's conception of junior and senior colleges, see Richard J. Storr, *Harper's University: The Beginnings* (Chicago: University of Chicago Press, 1966), pp. 117–20, 311–20.

10. William Rainey Harper, quoted in *The Chicago Tribune*, January 3, 1893, p. 3.

11. William Rainey Harper, "Convocation Address," September 30, 1894, Regenstein.

12. William Rainey Harper, "Address," October 1, 1894, Regenstein.

13. William Rainey Harper, "The Schools of Law and Medicine," *The Quarterly Calendar* 3 (1894): 16.

14. Ibid., p. 16.

15. *University Weekly*, June 21, 1894, p. 9.

16. For biographical information on Ernst Freund, see "Ernst Freund—Pioneer of Administrative Law," *University of Chicago Law Review* 29 (1962): 755–81; Frederic Woodward, "Ernst Freund," *University Record* 19 (1933): 39–42; Arthur H. Kent, "Ernst Freund—Jurist and Social Scientist," *Journal of Political Economy* 41 (1933): 145–51; and Oscar Kraines, *The World and Ideas of Ernst Freund: The Search for General Principles of Legislation and Administrative Law* (University, Alabama: The University of Alabama Press, 1974).

17. Felix Frankfurter, *Some Observations on Supreme Court Litigation and Legal Education*, The Ernst Freund Lectures (Chicago: University of Chicago Press, 1954), p. 1.

18. Ibid., p. 2.

19. Ernst Freund, "Law School and University," *University Record* 18 (1932): 149.

20. Ibid., pp. 148–49.

21. Woodward, "Freund," p. 35.

22. Freund, "Law School," p. 149.

23. Ibid., p. 152.

24. Freund to Harper, January 31, 1895, Regenstein.

25. March 6, 1897, Minutes of the University Senate, Regenstein.

26. William Rainey Harper, "Statement of the President," *Record* 2 (1897): 14.

27. Hamilton to Harper, May 10, 1898, Regenstein.

28. Adelbert Hamilton, *Suggestions as to Organizing a Law Department in the University of Chicago* (Chicago: Barnard & Miller, 1898).

29. Ibid., pp. 1, 2.

30. Ibid., pp. 2, 3.

31. Ibid., pp. 4, 5.

32. Ibid., pp. 7, 8.

33. Ibid., p. 13.
34. Ibid., pp. 15, 16.
35. Ibid., p. 18, tabulation 2.
36. Ibid., tabulation 3.
37. Ibid., tabulation 4.
38. Ibid., p. 23.
39. Ibid., pp. 24–28.
40. Ibid., p. 31.
41. Ibid.
42. William Rainey Harper, "Statement of the President," *Record* 4 (1899): 14.
43. Ibid., pp. 14–15.

Notes to Chapter Three

1. C. C. Kohlsaat to Harper, July 5, 1900, Regenstein.
2. Ibid.
3. Ibid.
4. William Rainey Harper, "The President's Quarterly Statement," *University Record* 6 (1902): 307.
5. William Rainey Harper, *The University Record* 7 (1903): 199.
6. William S. Pattee, "Law School of the University of Minnesota," *The Green Bag* 2 (1890): 204.
7. See "Academic Polity: the President and the Professors," in Richard J. Storr, *Harper's University: The Beginnings* (Chicago: University of Chicago Press, 1966), pp. 86–105.
8. William Rainey Harper, "Quarterly Statement," *Record* 1 (1896): 384.
9. George E. MacLean, "The Relation of Professional Schools to College Work," *University Record* 6 (1901–02): 3, 31.
10. Quoted in Joseph H. Beale, Jr., "The Place of Professional Education in the Universities," *University Record* 9 (1905): 42.
11. Ibid.
12. MacLean, "Relation of Professional Schools," p. 31.
13. Ernst Freund, "Circular of Information, Calendar for 1902–03, University of Chicago Law School," Regenstein, pp. 3, 8.
14. William Rainey Harper, *The University Record* 7 (1902–3): lxxxi.
15. Harper to Freund, April 24, 1901, Regenstein.
16. Freund to Harper, April 24, 1901, Regenstein.
17. Harper to Freund, April 31, 1901, Regenstein. It is not clear when it was discovered that Harper had cancer. After an appendectomy in May 1904, an examination of tissue revealed cancerous growth. See Storr, *Harper's University*, pp. 331, 359, 363–68.
18. Freund to Harper, December 3, 1901, Regenstein.
19. It was Keener who had triggered the 1891 revolution at Columbia Law School and who brought the Harvard case system

there, much to the unhappiness of the disciples of Theodore W. Dwight. See Julius Goebel, *A History of The School of Law, Columbia University* (New York: Columbia University Press, 1955), pp. 135–86.

20. Freund to Harper, December 3, 1901.

21. Ibid. The other men mentioned by Freund were Edward A. Harriman, who had just left Northwestern; Francis M. Burdick, professor at Columbia; Edwin Woodruff from Cornell; Frederic J. Stinson, author of *American Statute Law;* Stewart Chaplin, author of treatises on wills and trusts; Thaddeus K. Kenneson from New York University; Everett V. Abbott, who was teaching at Stanford; A. van Vechlen Veeder; Jesse M. Lilienthal; Gustavus Wald, editor of *Pollock's Contracts;* and Charles M. Hepburn, author of a treatise on code pleading.

22. See "Ernst Freund—Pioneer of Administrative Law," *The University of Chicago Law Review* 29 (1962): 755–81.

23. For biographical information on Beale, see *The University Record* 7 (1902–3): 201–2; Samuel Williston, "Joseph Henry Beale: A Biographical Sketch," *Harvard Law Review* 56 (1943): 686–89; Roscoe Pound, "Joseph Henry Beale," *Harvard Law Review* 56 (1943): 695–98; and Felix Frankfurter, "Joseph Henry Beale," *Harvard Law Review* 56 (1943): 701–03.

24. Williston, "Beale," p. 685.

25. Both men died in 1943. The March and October issues of the *Harvard Law Review* in that year contain dedications to these two men.

26. Williston, "Beale," p. 686.

27. Upon his return to Cambridge from Chicago in 1904, Beale's interest in politics increased. In 1907 he was elected to the board of aldermen. The *Boston Traveler* noted on December 12, 1970, that he was "the noted logician of the law school. He is popular throughout the city, and more than once his name has been suggested for mayor." Three years later, on February 12, the *Cambridge Chronicle* complimented Beale: "The public does not look askance as it did once when a Harvard professor's name is mentioned in connection with political office."

28. The *Boston Budget*, in discussing Harper's consideration of Beale as dean, on February 23, 1902, recorded that "Dr. Harper says that Prof. James Barr Ames, the present dean of Harvard Law School, is not being considered in connection with the new school."

29. Harper to Freund, January 9, 1902, Regenstein.

30. Anderson to Harper, February 17, 1902, Regenstein.

31. Ibid.

32. Edward H. Levi to the author, August 2, 1973.

33. *University Record* 7 (1902–3): lxxx.

34. Minutes of the Board of Trustees, January 21, 1902, Regenstein. Prior to this meeting the trustees showed no interest in re-

gard to the question of a law school, at least as expressed officially
in the minutes. Extensive discussions had occurred at trustee meetings concerning Rush Medical School, the School of Education, and
technological education, but there are no discussions of legal education on record.

35. Minutes of the Board of Trustees, March 14, 1902, Regenstein.

36. Ibid.

37. Ibid.

38. March 31, 1902, Minutes of the Harvard Corporation, Harvard University Archives.

39. William Rainey Harper, March 14, 1902, Minutes.

40. William Rainey Harper, "The President's Quarterly Statement," *The University Record* 6 (1902): 307, 308.

41. Ibid., p. 308.

42. John D. Rockefeller, Jr. to Andrew McLeish, February 20,
1902, incorporated into the March 11, 1902, Trustee Minutes.

43. William Rainey Harper quoted in Williston, "Beale," p. 687.
It is clear that Beale acknowledged that he had not been singled out
initially. Later Beale was to write, in discussing the initial luncheon
meeting with Harper, that "we talked over the possibility of my
going and by President Eliot's desire we tried to make arrangements
by which if you still needed one of us, he could be spared for a
couple of years." Beale to Harper, March 17, 1902, Regenstein.

44. Harper to Beale, March 14, 1902, Regenstein.

45. Ibid.

46. Beale to Harper, March 17, 1902.

47. Ibid.

48. Ibid.

49. Ibid.

50. Beale to Harper, March 27, 1902, Regenstein. Apparently the
argument submitted by Harper to Beale was that of a part-time arrangement for the first year, rather than a full two-year leave of
absence. Beale agreed to come for one-half of the academic year
1902–3.

51. F. W. Shepardson to Freund, March 26, 1902, Regenstein.

52. Harper to Freund, March 28, 1902, Regenstein. "On coming
home, I find your letter to me directed to Cambridge which reached
there after I had left and which was returned to me by Mr. Beale.
I regret I did not have the benefit of your instructions." Freund to
Harper, 1 April 1902, Regenstein.

53. Freund, "Circular of Information," p. 1.

54. Ibid., pp. 1–2.

55. Ibid., pp. 3–4.

56. Ibid., p. 8.

57. Ames to Harper, March 31, 1902, Regenstein.

58. Beale to Harper, April 2, 1902, Regenstein.

59. Ames to Harper, March 31, 1902.

60. Ibid.

61. Beale to Harper, April 2, 1902.

62. Ames to Harper, March 31, 1902.

63. Beale to Harper, April 2, 1902.

64. Ibid.

65. Ibid.

66. Ibid.

67. Ames to Harper, March 31, 1902.

68. Ibid. The writings and casebook of Freund are adequate evidence that he believed in the case method. The point which he was attempting to make was that the case method should not be viewed as the exclusive method, particularly after the middle of the student's second year. See "Freund, Pioneer of Administrative Law," pp. 768–69.

69. Ames to Harper, March 31, 1902.

70. Ibid.

71. Beale to Harper, April 2, 1902.

72. Ibid.

73. Ames to Harper, March 31, 1902.

Notes to Chapter Four

1. Beale to Harper, April 1, 1902, Regenstein.

2. Ibid.

3. Ernst Freund, *The University Record* 14 (1904–1905): 41.

4. Beale to Eliot, November 5, 1903, in Harvard University Archives, Widener Memorial Library (this source hereafter cited as Widener).

5. Edward H. Levi to the author, August 2, 1973.

6. Harper to Beale, April 9, 1902, Regenstein.

7. Beale to Harper, April 5, 1903, Regenstein.

8. Harper to Beale, April 8, 1903, Regenstein.

9. For further biographical information on Mack see August W. Hand, "Julian W. Mack," *Harvard Law Review* 57 (1943): 96–97. A recent biography of Mack by Harry Morton concentrates on Mack's role in the social reform movements in Chicago but does not deal at any length with Mack as lawyer, teacher, or judge—three areas in which Mack distinguished himself. *The Forging of an American Jew: The Life and Times of Judge Julian W. Mack* (New York: Herzl Press, 1974).

10. Lee to Eliot, March 15, 1897, and March 30, 1897, Widener.

11. Harper to Mechem, March 24, 1902, Regenstein.

12. For further biographical information on Mechem see Henry C. Adams, "Professor Floyd R. Mechem," publisher and date of publication unknown, probably a publication of the University of Michigan, while Mechem was still there.

13. Quoted in ibid.

14. Floyd R. Mechem, "The Opportunities and Responsibilities of American Law Schools," *Michigan Law Review* 5 (1902): 349.

15. Ibid., pp. 348, 349.

16. Ibid., pp. 347, 348.

17. Adams, "Mechem."

18. Mechem, "Opportunities and Responsibilities," p. 350.

19. Adams, "Mechem."

20. Mechem to Harper, April 3, 1902, Regenstein.

21. Harper to Mechem, April 5, 1902, Regenstein.

22. Ibid.

23. Mechem to Harper, April 11, 1902, Regenstein.

24. Both telegram drafts to Mechem from Harper are dated March 24, 1902, Regenstein.

25. Mechem to Harper, April 24, 1902, Regenstein.

26. Mechem to Harper, April 20, 1902, Regenstein.

27. Mechem to Harper, April 30, 1902, Regenstein.

28. Beale to Harper, June 21, 1903, Regenstein.

29. Harper to Beale, April 25, 1902, Regenstein.

30. Harper to Hall, April 11, 1902, Regenstein.

31. Hall to Harper, April 19, 1902, Regenstein.

32. Harper to Hall, no date, probably around April 21, 1902, Regenstein.

33. Charles Eliot to Hall, no date, probably in mid-April, 1902, Widener.

34. Hall to Harper, April 21, 1903, Regenstein.

35. Hall to Eliot, April 15, 1902, Widener.

36. Hall to Harper, April 21, 1902, Regenstein.

37. Ames to Eliot, April 30, 1902, Widener.

38. Jordan to Harper, April 24, 1902, Regenstein.

39. Harper to Jordan, April 30, 1902, Regenstein.

40. Beale to Harper, April 22, 1902, Regenstein.

41. Ames to Eliot, August 7, 1903, Widener.

42. Ames to Eliot, September 1, 1903, Widener.

43. Ames to Eliot, August 7, 1903, Widener.

44. Trustee Minutes, May 2, 1904, Regenstein. There were continued arguments during the early years of the Law School concerning law faculty salaries and promotion in relation to other parts of the university. Beale and later Hall urged for special treatment in view of the competition for faculty from the bar as well as from other schools. See in particular James Parker Hall to William Rainey Harper, "Memorandum Regarding Promotion from Associate Professorship to Full Professorship in the Law School," February 19, 1904, Regenstein.

45. On his letter of August 7, 1903, from Ames, Eliot drew a chart comparing the salaries of the law faculty with those of the Arts and Sciences faculty, indicating his concern for the differentia-

tion, which was $500 less in all categories for the latter. No top salary is given for either faculty.

46. Ames to Eliot, August 7, 1903, Widener.
47. Ames to Eliot, September 1, 1903, Widener.
48. Harper to Hall, April 29, 1902, Regenstein.
49. Beale to Harper, April 2, 1903, Regenstein.
50. Harper to Whittier, April 28, 1903, Regenstein.
51. Beale to Harper, April 22, 1902, Regenstein.
52. Trustee Minutes, May 1, 1903, Regenstein.
53. Law School Faculty Minutes, April 17, 1903, Regenstein.

Notes to Chapter Five

1. William Rainey Harper, "The School of Law," *University Record* 6 (1901–2): 389–90.
2. Ibid., p. 390.
3. William Rainey Harper, *Annual Register: Bulletin of Information, July 1901–July 1902* (Chicago: University of Chicago Press, 1902), p. 103.
4. Julius Goebel, *A History of The School of Law, Columbia University* (New York: Columbia University Press, 1955), pp. 85–89.
5. Ames to Eliot, August 1, 1900, Widener.
6. Ibid.
7. Richard J. Storr, *Harper's University: The Beginnings* (Chicago: University of Chicago Press, 1966), p. 76, see pp. 74–77.
8. Max Rheinstein, "Law Faculties and Law Schools: A Comparison of Legal Education in the United States and Germany," *Wisconsin Law Review* 13 (1938): 58. See also Stefan Riesenfeld, "A Comparison of Continental and American Legal Education," *Michigan Law Review* 36 (1937): 31–55; Simeon E. Baldwin, "Graduate Courses at Law Schools," *Journal of Social Science* 11 (1880): 123–37; Gerhard Casper, "Two Models of Legal Education," *Tennessee Law Review* 51 (1973): 13–25; and Edward V. Raynolds, "Legal Education in Germany," *Yale Law Journal* 12 (1902): 31–34.
9. In his study of "Two Models of Legal Education," Gerhard Casper notes that the influence of Roman law on the Continent was so profound that it "dominated legal education, at least in Germany, until well into the nineteenth century." With the growth in scientific study toward the end of the nineteenth century in the universities, Casper observes, "the links between the study of law and theology, philosophy, history and politics were ruptured by the trend toward scientific specialization, ever spreading since at least the end of the eighteenth century" (p. 15).
10. Rheinstein, "Law Faculties and Law Schools," p. 13.
11. James Parker Hall, *University Record* 9 (1903–4): 367.
12. Minutes of the University Senate, March 1, 1902, Regenstein.
13. The information on the faculty and curriculum for these de-

partments is taken from *Annual Register: Bulletin of Information, July, 1900–July, 1901* (Chicago: University of Chicago Press, 1901).

14. Law Faculty Minutes, April 15, 1902, Regenstein.

15. Blewett Lee, "Teaching Practice in Law Schools," *Report of the 1896 Annual Meeting of the American Bar Association* (1896), 507–8, 508–9.

16. Ibid., pp. 510, 511, 512.

17. Ibid., p. 520.

18. William Rainey Harper, *University Record* 7 (1902–3): 200.

19. University Council Minutes, January 6, 1906; January 10, 1906; January 16, 1906; and January 20, 1906; Regenstein.

20. University Council Minutes, November 10, 1905, Regenstein. A course of instruction that met daily, i.e., four or five days a week throughout the quarter, was called a major. A course which met daily for half the quarter was called a minor. These definitions were applicable to all university courses.

21. University Council Minutes, November 20, 1905.

22. About forty members of other law faculties visited Chicago through 1915. A complete list can be found in James Parker Hall, "The Law School," *President's Report, 1915–1916* (Chicago: University of Chicago Press, 1917). See also James Parker Hall, "The Law School—a Review," *University of Chicago Magazine* 7 (1915): 69–76.

23. Edward H. Levi to the author, August 2, 1973.

24. Law Faculty Minutes, November 7, 1902, Regenstein.

25. James Parker Hall, *The University Record* 8 (1903–4): 57–58.

26. James Parker Hall, "The Law School," *President's Report, 1906–1907* (Chicago: University of Chicago Press, 1907), p. 36.

27. Trustee Minutes, January 21, 1902, Regenstein.

28. "The Law School: Provisional Statement," Minutes of the University Senate, March 1, 1902, Regenstein.

29. Law Faculty Minutes, April 16, 1902, Regenstein.

30. William Rainey Harper, *The Trend in Higher Education* (Chicago: University of Chicago Press, 1905), p. 84.

31. Ibid., p. 345.

32. Ibid., p. 346.

33. Ibid.

34. Beale to Eliot, May 19, 1905, Widener.

35. Nicholas Murray Butler, "The Length of the College Course," in Charles Eliot, et al. *Present College Questions* (New York: D. Appleton and Co., 1903), pp. 98–99.

36. Ibid., p. 104. Cf. Andrew F. West, "The Length of the College Course," in ibid. West was dean of the Graduate School at Princeton.

37. For a discussion of Harper's attempts to separate the junior college from the Midway and for the curricula of the junior and

senior college, see Storr, *Harper's University*, pp. 117–28; 305–26.

38. *Annual Register, 1901–1902*, p. 363.

39. William Rainey Harper, *The University Record* 9 (1904–1905): 57.

Notes to Chapter Six

1. Beale to Harper, March 17, 1902, Regenstein.

2. Law Faculty Minutes, April 15, 1902, Regenstein.

3. James Parker Hall, "The Law School: A Review," *University of Chicago Magazine* 7 (1914): 72.

4. Joseph H. Beale, "The Place of Professional Education in the Universities," *University Record* 9 (1905): 46.

5. Mack to Harper, July 30, 1902, Regenstein.

6. Freund to Harper, July 20, 1902, Regenstein.

7. Beale to Harper, August 12, 1902, Regenstein.

8. Harper to Beale, August 15, 1902, Regenstein.

9. Beale to Harper, October 4, 1902, Regenstein.

10. Ibid.

11. Beale to Eliot, November 5, 1903, Widener. Acknowledged for Eliot by Jerome D. Greene to Joseph H. Beale, December 23, 1903, Regenstein.

12. For a discussion of the establishment of the library, see Hall, "Law School Review," pp. 72–74. See also the *Annual Register, 1902–1903*. (Chicago: University of Chicago Press, 1903), pp. 103–04.

13. Mack to Harper, July 30, 1905, Regenstein.

14. Beale to Harper, March 17, 1902, Regenstein.

15. James Barr Ames to Charles Eliot, August 31, 1903, Widener.

16. James Parker Hall to William Rainey Harper, January 27, 1904, Regenstein.

17. *Annual Register, 1901–1903*, p. 103. The early *Announcements* of the Law School are found in the *Annual Register*.

18. Ibid.

19. See Richard J. Storr, *Harper's University: The Beginnings* (Chicago: University of Chicago Press, 1966), p. 77.

20. *The Maroon*, October 1, 1902.

21. Ibid., October 2, 1902.

22. William Rainey Harper, *The University Record* 7 (1902–3): 199.

23. Ibid.

24. Ernst Freund, "The Correlation of Work for Higher Degrees in Graduate School and Law School," *Illinois Law Review* 11 (1916): 301.

25. Harper, *Record* (1902–3), p. lxxxiii.

26. Freund, "Correlation of Work," pp. 69–70.

27. James Parker Hall, "American Law School Degrees," *Michigan Law Review* 6 (1907): 113, 114.

28. Hall, "Law School Review," pp. 69–70.

29. Minutes of the University Senate, March 1, 1902; Trustee Minutes, May 1, 1902; and Law Faculty Minutes, Regenstein.

30. *The Annual Register, 1901–1902*, p. 98.

31. *The Annual Register, 1902–1903*, p. 102.

32. Toward the end of his term as dean, Ames pushed Eliot, who was not moved. In a letter to Eliot, on December 3, 1908, Ames said: "The Law Faculty of the Harvard Law School would be glad to substitute this degree for the degree of LL.B." (Widener).

33. Chandler to Hall, June 7, 1906, Regenstein.

34. Hall to Chandler, June 9, 1906, Regenstein.

35. Law Faculty Minutes, August 7, 1902, Regenstein.

36. *The Annual Register, 1902–1903*, p. 103. From 1902 to 1914, 364 J.D. degrees were conferred (92 cum laude) and 63 LL.B. degrees (14 cum laude). The faculty voted to grant degrees with honors in 1904.

37. Harper, *Record* (1902–3), p. 240.

38. *The Annual Register, 1902–1903*, pp. 102–5.

39. *The Annual Register, 1903–1904*, pp. 103–6.

40. Frederick R. Baird to the author, March 17, 1972.

41. Edward J. Clark to the author, March 11, 1973.

42. Albrecht R.C. Kipp to the author, March 3, 1972.

43. Beale to Eliot, November 5, 1903, Widener.

44. William Rainey Harper, *The University Record* (1903–4), p. 38.

45. Beatrice Doerschuk, *Women in the Law* (New York: Bureau of Vocational Information, 1920), bull. no. 3, pp. 19–25. See also Cynthia F. Epstein, "Women and Professional Cases: The Case of the Woman Lawyer" (Ph.D. dissertation, Columbia University, 1968).

46. Frederick C. Hicks, *Yale Law School: 1869–1894, Including The County Court House Period*, Yale Law Library Publications, no. 4 (New Haven: Yale University Press, 1937) p. 72.

47. Ibid., pp. 74–75.

48. The struggle for admission of women presented problems for Columbia, although at a later time. In 1924 the National League of Women Voters and other groups urged that women be admitted. Columbia responded by claiming that this concession would be "inexpedient and contrary to the best interests of the Law School." In 1927 the faculty agreed to allow Barnard College graduates to be admitted, although Karl N. Llewellyn emphasized that the women would have to meet the same standards for admission as the men. Finally in 1928 the policy of "deliberate antifeminism" was eliminated completely, and the Columbia faculty adjusted to a policy which after a discussion period of four years was now deemed

expedient and in their best interests. See Julius Goebel, *A History of The School of Law, Columbia University* (New York: Columbia University Press, 1955), pp. 290–91.

49. Document undated, Widener.

50. Doreschuk, *Women*, pp. 19–25.

51. William Rainey Harper, *The Trend in Higher Education* (Chicago: University of Chicago Press, 1905), pp. 301, 311.

52. Marion Talbot, *More than Lore* (Chicago: University of Chicago Press, 1936), pp. 175.

53. Eileen Markely Znaniecki, to the author, April 5, 1972.

54. *Cap and Gown* (Chicago: University of Chicago Press, 1904), p. 175.

55. See the 1903, 1904, and 1905 issues of *Cap and Gown*, all published by the University of Chicago Press.

56. *The Maroon*, November 18 and 21, 1902 .

57. James W. Thompson, "The House System of the University," *President's Report, 1892–1902* (Chicago: University of Chicago Press, 1902), p. 387. See Storr, *Harper's University*, p. 321.

58. Harper, *Record* (1902–3), p. 241.

59. *The Maroon*, October 6, 9, and November 18, 1903.

60. Erwin N. Griswold, *Law and Lawyers in the United States* (Cambridge: Harvard University Press, 1964), pp. 53–54.

61. Hall to Ernest D. Burton, March 7, 1924, Regenstein.

62. Mack to Harper, November 6, 1903, Regenstein.

63. Harper to Hall, May 23, 1904, Regenstein.

64. See *The President's Report, 1902–1904* (Chicago: University of Chicago Press, 1904), pp. 242–43; 255–56; 267; Trustee Minutes, March 31, 1903, Regenstein.

65. See *The President's Report, 1904–1905* (Chicago: University of Chicago Press, 1905), p. 159.

66. See *The President's Report, 1909–1910* (Chicago: University of Chicago Press, 1910), p. 187.

67. Minutes of the University Senate, January 4, 1902, Regenstein.

68. Trustee Minutes, April 15, 1902, Regenstein.

69. Trustee Minutes, May 1, 1902, Regenstein.

70. Swift to Rockefeller, January 15, 1935, Regenstein.

71. Rockefeller to Harold W. Swift, January 21, 1935, Regenstein.

72. Trustee Minutes, August 19, 1902, Regenstein.

73. "Report of the Committee on the Placing of Buildings for Instruction and Research," in Senate Minutes, May 3, 1902, Regenstein.

74. Ibid.

75. University Council Minutes, May 31, 1902, Regenstein.

76. For descriptions of the building after completion, see *The University of Chicago Official Guide* (Chicago: University of Chicago Press, 1916), pp. 80–82; Note Flint, *The University of Chicago*

(Chicago: University of Chicago Press, 1904), pp. 24–25; and Thomas Wakefield Goodspeed, *A History of The University of Chicago* (Chicago: University of Chicago Press, 1916), pp. 350–52.

77. For information on the bids, see W. J. Cooledge to Henry A. Rust, January 16, 1903, Regenstein.

78. William Rainey Harper, *The University Record* 8 (1903–4): 38.

79. Harper, quoted in Hall, "Law School Review," p. 71.

80. Beale to Harper, August 12, 1902; Harper to Beale, August 15, 1902; Regenstein.

81. *Maroon*, October 1, 1902.

82. *Maroon*, October 2, 1902.

83. Ibid.

84. Harper, *Record* (1902–3), p. 241.

Bibliography

I. Unpublished Material

A. Materials found in Special Collections, The Joseph Regenstein Library, University of Chicago

1. *Private Papers, University Records, Manuscripts*

The following collections contain documents used in this study.

The Presidents' Papers, 1889–1925. Includes items on the Law School, business manager, Ernst Freund, trustees, and miscellaneous items (PP).

University Administrative Boards and Bodies. Contains Law School faculty minutes, 1902–38, University Senate minutes, 1896–1902, and the University Council minutes, 1892–1908 (AB&B).

The Ernst Freund Papers.

The Board of Trustees. Includes correspondence of the secretary of the Board, 1890–1913, and minutes of the meetings of the board, 1890–1912 (T).

Committee of the Board of Trustees on Buildings and Grounds, 1892–1912. Contains information on the old Law School building (B&G).

Thomas Wakefield Goodspeed Papers (TG).

Frederick T. Gates Papers.

William Rainey Harper Personal Papers.

Richard Storr Papers.

The Correspondence of the Founder and Associates (FA).

The following items from the above collections were used in this study.

Adams, Henry C. "Professor Floyd R. Mechem." Date of publication not known; it appears to have been published by the University of Michigan while Mechem was still there (PP).

Azelin, Arthur A. "The Old University of Chicago." D.B. paper, University of Chicago, 1941.

"Circular of Information, The School of Law of the University of Chicago, founded by John D. Rockefeller." Calendar for the year 1902–3 (PP).

Goodspeed, Thomas Wakefield. "Reminiscences of Thomas Wakefield Goodspeed" (TG).

Harper, William Rainey. "Address." October 1, 1894 (PP).

———. "Convocation Address." September 30, 1894 (PP).

Koenitzer, C. H. "History of the First University of Chicago, 1856–1886." 1927 or 1928.

Law Faculty Minutes. April 15, 16, August 7, October 2, and November 7, 1902; May 9, 1903 (AB&B).

"The Law School: Provisional Statement." March 1, 1902 (AB&B).

Lawrence, Thomas J. "Memorial on the Creation of a Law School in the University of Chicago." January 2, 1893 (PP).

"Report of the Committee on the Placing of Buildings for Instruction and Research." May 3, 1902 (AB&B).

"Report of the Conference between Messrs. F. T. Gates, T. W. Goodspeed, and H. A. Rust, with Reference to the University of Chicago." February 10, 1897 (FA).

Trustee Minutes. January 21, April 15, March 11, May 1, August 19, 1902; March 31, 1903 (T).

University Council Minutes. May 31, 1902; November 20, December 2, 1905; January 6, 10, 16, and 20, 1902 (AB&B).

2. Letters

The following letters are found in the Presidents' Papers, 1889–1925, unless otherwise noted.

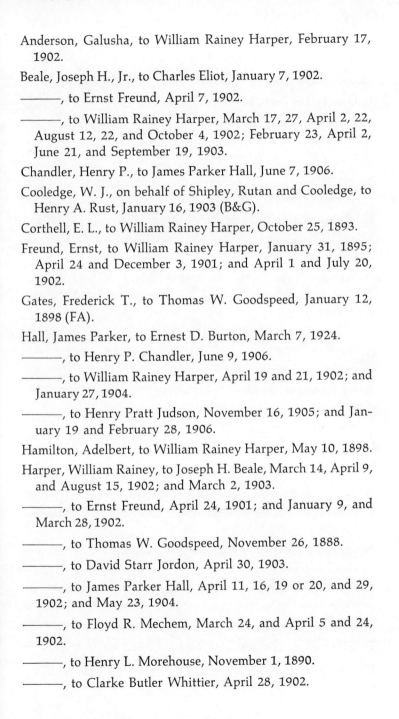

Anderson, Galusha, to William Rainey Harper, February 17, 1902.

Beale, Joseph H., Jr., to Charles Eliot, January 7, 1902.

————, to Ernst Freund, April 7, 1902.

————, to William Rainey Harper, March 17, 27, April 2, 22, August 12, 22, and October 4, 1902; February 23, April 2, June 21, and September 19, 1903.

Chandler, Henry P., to James Parker Hall, June 7, 1906.

Cooledge, W. J., on behalf of Shipley, Rutan and Cooledge, to Henry A. Rust, January 16, 1903 (B&G).

Corthell, E. L., to William Rainey Harper, October 25, 1893.

Freund, Ernst, to William Rainey Harper, January 31, 1895; April 24 and December 3, 1901; and April 1 and July 20, 1902.

Gates, Frederick T., to Thomas W. Goodspeed, January 12, 1898 (FA).

Hall, James Parker, to Ernest D. Burton, March 7, 1924.

————, to Henry P. Chandler, June 9, 1906.

————, to William Rainey Harper, April 19 and 21, 1902; and January 27, 1904.

————, to Henry Pratt Judson, November 16, 1905; and January 19 and February 28, 1906.

Hamilton, Adelbert, to William Rainey Harper, May 10, 1898.

Harper, William Rainey, to Joseph H. Beale, March 14, April 9, and August 15, 1902; and March 2, 1903.

————, to Ernst Freund, April 24, 1901; and January 9, and March 28, 1902.

————, to Thomas W. Goodspeed, November 26, 1888.

————, to David Starr Jordon, April 30, 1903.

————, to James Parker Hall, April 11, 16, 19 or 20, and 29, 1902; and May 23, 1904.

————, to Floyd R. Mechem, March 24, and April 5 and 24, 1902.

————, to Henry L. Morehouse, November 1, 1890.

————, to Clarke Butler Whittier, April 28, 1902.

Hopkins, George G., to William Rainey Harper, March 13, 1893.

Jordon, David Starr, to William Rainey Harper, April 24, 1902.

Judson, Henry Pratt, to Joseph H. Beale, Jr., May 9, 1910.

Lawrence, Thomas J., to William Rainey Harper, February 29, 1892.

Kohlsaat, C. C., to William Rainey Harper, July 5, 1900.

Mack, Julian W., to William Rainey Harper, July 30, 1902; and November 6, 1903.

Mathews, Shailer, to Henry Pratt Judson, February 26, 1906.

Mechem, Floyd R., to William Rainey Harper, April 3, 11, 24, and 30, 1902.

Rockefeller, John D., Jr., to Andrew McLeish, February 20, 1902, in the March 11, 1902, Minutes of the Board of Trustees (T).

————, to Harold H. Swift, January 21, 1935, in President's Papers, 1925–45.

Shepardson, F. W., to Ernst Freund, March 26, 1902.

Swift, Harold H., to John D. Rockefeller, Jr., January 15, 1935, in Presidents' Papers, 1925–45.

B. Materials found in Harvard University Archives, The Widener Library

Ames, James Barr, to Charles Eliot, August 1, 1900; April 30, and August 31, 1902; September 1 and August 7, 1903; and December 3, 1908.

Beale, Joseph H., Jr., to Charles Eliot, November 5, 1903; and May 19, 1905.

Eliot, Charles, to James Parker Hall, no date, but probably in early April 1902.

Hall, James Parker, to Charles Eliot, April 15, 1902.

Lee, Blewett, to Charles Eliot, March 15 and 30, 1897.

Minutes of the Harvard Corporation. March 31, 1902.

C. Dissertations and Theses

Engle, Gale W. "William Rainey Harper's Conception of the Structuring of the Functions Performed by the Educational Institutions." Ph.D. dissertation, Stanford University, 1954.

Epstein, Cynthia F. "Women and Professional Careers: The Case of the Woman Lawyer." Ph.D. dissertation, Columbia University, 1968.

Gawalt, Gerard W. "Massachusetts Lawyers: A Historical Analysis of the Process of Professionalization, 1760–1840." Ph.D. dissertation, Clark University, 1969.

Haggerty, William James. "The Purpose of the University of Chicago." Ph.D. dissertation, University of Chicago, 1943.

Hales, William H. "The Career Development of the Negro Lawyer in Chicago." Ph.D. dissertation, University of Chicago, 1949.

Ingersoll, David Edward. "Karl Llewellyn and American Legal Realism." Ph.D. dissertation, Claremont Graduate School, 1964.

Joy, Aryness. "Professional Organization of Lawyers in the United States." Ph.D. dissertation, University of Chicago, 1924.

Katz, Joseph. "The Legal Profession, 1890–1915, The Lawyer's Role in Society: A Study of Attitude." Master's Thesis, Columbia University, 1953.

Lortie, D. C. "The Striving Young Lawyer. A Study of Early Career Differentiation in the Chicago Bar." Ph.D. dissertation, University of Chicago, 1958.

McKirdy, Charles R. "Lawyers in Crisis: The Massachusetts Legal Profession, 1760–1790." Ph.D. dissertation, Northwestern University, 1969.

Rutherford, Mary Louise Schuman. "The Influence of the American Bar Association on Public Opinion and Legislation." Ph.D. dissertation, University of Pennsylvania, 1936.

Sommers, Lawrence Edmund. "Lawyers and Progressive Reform: A Study of Attitudes and Activities in Illinois, 1890 to 1920." Ph.D. dissertation, Northwestern University, 1967.

D. Other Materials

1. The following items, found in the library at Northwestern University and cited in James A. Rahl and Kurt Schwerin, *Northwestern University School of Law: A Short History*, which was privately printed in Chicago in 1960, were used in the study.

Childs, Frank H., to Dr. D. M. Sommerville, April 5, 1939.

"Northwestern University Law School, Circular of Information," 1891–92; "Alumni Association, Union College of Law, Alumni, Officers, and Instructors," 1859–90.

Northwestern University Board of Trustee Minutes. June 21, 1854; June 6 and 7, 1857; June 29, 1858; March 5 and April 4, 1859; June 24, 1873; June 23, 1874; June 20, 1876; June 20 and July 21, 1891; and July 11, 1895.

Records of the Faculty. Northwestern University School of Law, June 8, 1894.

Wigmore, John Henry. "Northwestern University School of Law, Educational Survey, 1927, Report of the Dean." Mimeographed report in seven parts.

2. *Letters to the author*

Baird, Frederick R., March 17, 1972.

Clark, Edward J., March 11, 1973.

Kipp, Albrecht R. C., March 3, 1972.

Levi, Edward H., August 2, 1973.

Tefft, Sheldon, July 17, 1973.

Znaniecki, Eileen Markely, April 5, 1972.

II. Published Material

A. Articles, Books, and other printed material concerning the University of Chicago, including the old University of Chicago

Alumni Directory, The University of Chicago, 1861–1910. Chicago: University of Chicago Press, 1910.

Cap and Gown. Chicago: University of Chicago Press, 1903–5.

Cuppy, Will J. *Maroon Tales: University of Chicago Stories.* Chicago: Forbes & Company, 1910.

The First Fifty Years: Commemorating The University of Chicago's Fiftieth Anniversary, 1891–1941. N.p., n.d.

Flint, Nott. *The University of Chicago.* Chicago: University of Chicago Press, 1904.

Freund, Ernst. "Law School and University." *University Record* 18 (1932): 143–52.

General Register of the Officers and Alumni, 1892–1902. Chicago: University of Chicago Press, 1902.

Goodspeed, Thomas Wakefield. *A History of The University of Chicago.* Chicago: University of Chicago Press, 1916.

————. *The University of Chicago Biographical Sketches.* 2 vols. Chicago: University of Chicago Press, 1922, 1925.

————. *The Story of the University of Chicago.* Chicago: University of Chicago Press, 1925.

————. *William Rainey Harper.* Chicago: University of Chicago Press, 1928.

Hall, James Parker. "The Law School." *The President's Report, 1906–1907.* Chicago: University of Chicago Press, 1908.

————. "The Law School." *The President's Report, 1915–1916.* Chicago: University of Chicago Press, 1917.

————. "The Law School—A Review." *University of Chicago Magazine* 7 (1915): 69–76.

Hamilton, Adelbert. *Suggestions as to Organizing a Law Department in the University of Chicago.* Chicago: Barnard & Miller, 1898.

Harper, William Rainey. Interview quoted in *Chicago Tribune*, January 3, 1893, p. 3.

————. Interview quoted in *University Weekly*, October 26, 1893, p. 6.

————. "The President's Quarterly Statement." *University Record* 6 (1902): 307–08.

————. "The President's Forty-First Quarterly Statement." *University Record* 6 (1902): 389–90.

————. "Quarterly Statement of the President." *University Record* 1 (1896): 384.

————. "Quarterly Statement of the President." *University Record* 2 (1898): 322.

————. "The School of Law." *University Record* 6 (1901–2): 389–90.

————. "The Schools of Law and Medicine." *Quarterly Calendar* 3 (1894): 16.

————. "Statement of the President." *University Record* 2 (1898): 14.

————. "Statement of the President." *University Record* 4 (1900): 14.

————. *The University of Chicago, The First Annual Report, 1892.* Chicago: n.p., 1892.

Herrick, Robert. "The Aims of Chicago." *Scribner's Magazine* 18 (1895): 397–417.

"The Law School Alumni Association." *University of Chicago Magazine* 7 (1914): 86–92.

Maroon. October 1, 1902–October 1, 1906.

Official Bulletin No. 1. Chicago: University of Chicago Press, 1891.

Officers and Instructors, The University of Chicago Directory. Chicago: Phillips and Company, 1892.

The President's Report. Chicago: University of Chicago Press. *The President's Report*, which contains reports of deans and officers of the university, began in 1897–98 and lapsed until 1902 when it resumed publication and went on through 1910.

Publications of the Members of the University, 1902–1916. Chicago: University of Chicago Press, 1917.

Raney, M. Llewellyn. *The University Libraries. 7, The University of Chicago Survey.* Chicago: University of Chicago Press, 1933.

Annual Register. Chicago: University of Chicago Press, 1893–1904.

The Regulations of The University of Chicago. Chicago: University of Chicago Press, 1903.

Robertson, David Allan. *The Quarter-Centennial Celebration of the University of Chicago.* Chicago: University of Chicago Press, 1918.

Shepardson, Francis W. "An Historical Sketch." *President's Report, 1897–98.* Chicago: University of Chicago Press, 1899.

Storr, Richard J. *Harper's University: The Beginnings.* Chicago: University of Chicago Press, 1966.

Talbot, Marion. *More Than Lore.* Chicago: University of Chicago Press, 1936.

Tefft, Sheldon. "The Law School at the University of Chicago." *Oxonian* 50 (1963): 14–240.

University of Chicago Annual Catalogue. 1–27. Chicago: n.p., 1859–1860 through 1886–87. Catalogue of the old University of Chicago.

University of Chicago Convocation Programs. 42–83. Chicago: n.p., 1902–12.

The University of Chicago Law School Alumni Directory. Chicago: University of Chicago Press, 1968.

The University of Chicago Law School Alumni Directory, ed. Frank L. Ellsworth. Braintree, Mass.: Semline, Inc., 1974.

The University of Chicago Official Guide. Chicago: University of Chicago Press, 1916.

University Record. Chicago: University of Chicago Press, 1896–1906. The *University Record* superseded the *Quarterly Calendar* which was issued between 1892 and 1896 and contained Harper's quarterly statements and other information and reports on the university.

University Weekly. A student publication begun when the university was opened and superseded by the *Maroon*, which began as a daily newspaper October 1, 1902.

B. Books

Adams, John. *The Adams Papers, Diary and Autobiography*

of *John Adams*. Vol. 3. Cambridge: Harvard University Press, 1961.

Alvarez, A. *The Progress of Continental Law in the 19th Century*. The Continental Legal History Series, no. 11. Boston: Little, Brown, 1918.

Ames, James Barr. *Lectures on Legal Education*. Cambridge: Harvard University Press, 1913.

Anatomy of Modern Legal Education. St. Paul: West Publishing Company, 1961.

Annual Review of Legal Education (1913–34). 22 vols. New York: Carnegie Foundation, 1913–34.

Auerbach, Jerold S. *Unequal Justice: Lawyers and Social Change in Modern America*. New York: Oxford University Press, 1976.

Aumann, Francis R. *The Changing American Legal System: Some Selected Phases*. Columbus: Ohio State University Press, 1940.

Bailyn, Bernard. *Education in the Forming of American Society: Needs and Opportunities for Study*. Chapel Hill: University of North Carolina Press, 1960.

Baldwin, Simeon E. *The Young Man and The Law*. New York: Macmillan, 1920.

Bancroft, Hubert Howe. *The Book of the Fair: An Historical and Descriptive Presentation of the World's Science, Art, and Industry, as viewed through the Columbian Exposition at Chicago in 1893*. New York: Bounty Books, 1894.

Barnard, Harry. *The Forging of an American Jew: The Life and Times of Judge Julian Mack*. New York: Herzl Press, 1974.

Birks, Michael. *Gentleman of the Law*. London: Stevens & Sons, 1960.

Blauch, Lloyd E., ed. *Education for the Professions*. Washington: United States Office of Education, 1955.

Blaustein, Albert P., and Porter, Charles O. *The American Lawyer: A Summary of the Survey of the Legal Profession*. Chicago: University of Chicago Press, 1954.

Bloomfield, Maxwell. *American Lawyers in a Changing Society, 1776–1876*. Studies in Legal History. Cambridge: Harvard University Press, 1976.

Bonney, Charles Carroll. *World's Congress Addresses*, Chicago: Open Court Publishing Company, 1900.

Boorstin, Daniel J. *The Americans: The Colonial Experience*. New York: Random House, 1958.

Brown, Elizabeth Gaspar. *Legal Education at Michigan, 1859–1959*. Ann Arbor: University of Michigan Law School, 1959.

Brown, Esther Lucille. *Lawyers, Law Schools and the Public Service*. New York: Russell Sage Foundation, 1948.

———. *Lawyers and the Promotion of Justice*. New York: Russell Sage Foundation, 1938.

Brownell, Emery S. *Legal Aid in the United States*. Rochester: Lawyers Cooperative Publishing Company, 1951.

Brubacher, John S., and Rudy, Willis. *Higher Education in Transition: A History of American Colleges and Universities, 1936–1968*. New York: Harper & Row, 1968.

Burg, David F. *Chicago's White City of 1893*. Lexington: University Press of Kentucky, 1976.

Butts, R. Freeman, and Cremin, Lawrence A. *A History of Education in American Culture*. New York: Holt, 1953.

Cahn, Edward V. *The Moral Decision: Right and Wrong in the Light of American Law*. Bloomington: Indiana University Press, 1955.

Calhoun, Daniel H. *Professional Lives in America: Structure and Aspiration, 1750–1850*. Cambridge: Harvard University Press, 1965.

The Centennial History of the Harvard Law School. Cambridge: Harvard Law School Association, 1918.

Chicago Bar-Association Lectures. Chicago: Fergus Printing Company, 1882.

Choate, Joseph H. *Our Profession*. Chicago: American Bar Association, 1898.

Chroust, Anton-Hermann. *The Rise of the Legal Profession*. 2 vols. Norman: University of Oklahoma Press, 1965.

Cohen, Julius Henry. *Law—Business or Profession?* New York: Banks Law Publishing Company, 1916.

Conference on The Profession of Law and Legal Education. University of Chicago Law School Conference Series. Vol. 16. Chicago: University of Chicago Law School, 1952.

Coulter, Ellis M. *College Life in the Old South.* Athens: University of Georgia Press, 1951.

Cremin, Lawrence A. *The Transformation of The School: Progressivism in American Education, 1876–1957.* New York: Random House, 1961.

Cummings, Homer, and McFarland, Carl. *Federal Justice: Chapters in the History of Justice and the Federal Executive.* New York: DeCapo Press, 1937.

Curti, Merle. *The Social Ideas of American Educators.* Paterson, New Jersey: Littlefield, Adams and Company, 1959.

————, and Nash, Roderick. *Philanthropy in the Shaping of American Higher Education.* New Brunswick, New Jersey: Rutgers University Press, 1965.

Destler, Chester McArthur. *American Radicalism, 1865–1901, Essays and Documents.* New London: Connecticut College, 1946.

Dillon, John F. *The Laws and Jurisprudence of England and America.* Boston, 1894.

Doerschuk, Beatrice. *Women in the Law.* Bull. no. 3. New York: Bureau of Vocational Information, 1920.

Dos Passos, John R. *The American Lawyer, As He Is—As He Can Be.* New York: Banks Law Publishing Company, 1907.

Edwards, Newton, and Richey, Herman G. *The School in the American Social Order.* Boston: Houghton Mifflin, 1963.

Eliot, Charles; West, Andrew; Harper, William Rainey; and Butler, Nicholas Murray. *Present College Questions.* New York: D. Appleton and Company, 1903.

Flexner, Abraham. *Medical Education in the United States and Canada.* Bull. no. 4. New York: Carnegie Foundation for the Advancement of Teaching, 1910.

————. *Universities: American, English, German.* New York: Oxford University Press, 1930.

Frankfurter, Felix. *Some Observations on Supreme Court Litigation and Legal Education*. Chicago: University of Chicago Press, 1954.

Friedman, Lawrence M. *A History of American Law*. New York: Simon and Schuster, 1973.

Gavit, Bernard C. *Introduction to the Study of Law*. Brooklyn: Foundation Press, 1951.

Goebel, Julius. *A History of The School of Law, Columbia University*. New York: Columbia University Press, 1955.

Goldman, Marion S. *A Portrait of the Black Attorney in Chicago*. Chicago: American Bar Foundation, 1972.

Greenwood, Glenn, and Frederickson, Robert F. *Specialization in the Medical and Legal Professions*. Mundelein, Illinois: Callaghan & Company, 1964.

Greer, Thomas H. *American Social Reform Movements*. Englewood Cliffs, N.J.: Prentice-Hall, 1949.

Griswold, Erwin N. *Law and Lawyers in the United States*. Cambridge: Harvard University Press, 1964.

Hanbury, Harold G. *The Vinerian Chair and Legal Education*. Oxford: Blackwell, 1958.

Harno, Albert J. *Legal Education in the United States*. San Francisco: Bancroft-Whitney, 1953.

Harris, William T. *Report of the Commissioner of Education, 1890–91*. Washington, D.C.: Government Printing Office, 1894.

Harvard College, Class of 1882, 25th Anniversary Report. Boston: privately printed, 1897.

Harvard Law School Association. Report of the Ninth Annual Meeting, June 25, 1895, in Especial Honor of Christopher Columbus Langdell. Boston: Harvard Law School Association, 1895.

Herrick, Robert. *Chimes*. New York: Macmillan, 1926.

Hicks, Frederick C. *Yale Law School: 1869–1894. Including The County Court House Period*. Yale Law Library Publications, no. 4. New Haven: Yale University Press, 1937.

————. *Yale Law School: 1895–1915: Twenty Years of*

Hendrie Hall. Yale Law Library Publications, no. 7. New Haven: Yale University Press, 1937.

Hofstadter, Richard. *The Age of Reform.* New York: Random House, 1955.

————, and Metzger, Walter P. *The Development of Academic Freedom in the United States.* New York: Columbia University Press, 1955.

Horton, Olive H. *The Law School.* Vol. 4. *Northwestern University—A History, 1855–1905.* Edited by Arthur Herbert. New York: University Publishing Society, 1905.

Howe, Mark DeWolfe, ed. *Readings in American Legal History.* Cambridge: Harvard University Press, 1949.

Hughes, Everett C., and Gurin, Arnold. *Education for the Professions of Medicine, Law, Theology, and Social Welfare.* New York: McGraw-Hill, 1973.

Hurst, Willard. *The Growth of American Law: The Law Makers.* Boston: Little, Brown, 1950.

Jones, Howard Mumford. *The Age of Energy.* New York: Viking, 1971.

Karier, Clarence J. *Man, Society, and Education: A History of American Educational Ideas.* Chicago: Scott, Foresman, 1967.

Kogan, Herman. *The First Century: The Chicago Bar Association, 1874–1974.* Chicago: Rand McNally, 1974.

Kraines, Oscar. *The World and Ideas of Ernst Freund: The Search for General Principles of Legislation and Administrative Law.* University, Alabama: University of Alabama Press, 1974.

Langeluttig, Albert G. *The Department of Justice of the United States.* Baltimore: Johns Hopkins Press, 1927.

The Law Schools Look Ahead. Ann Arbor: Privately printed, 1959.

Lee, Alfred McClung. *The Daily Newspaper in America.* New York: Macmillan, 1937.

Llewellyn, Karl N. *The Bramble Bush: Our Law and Its Study.* Dobbs Ferry, New York: Oceana Press, 1951.

Martin, George. *Causes and Conflicts—the Centennial History of the Association of the Bar of the City of New York, 1870–1970*. Boston: Houghton Mifflin, 1970.

Mather, Cotton. *Bonifacius: an essay upon the good* (1710). Ed. David Levin, Cambridge: Harvard University Press, Belknap Press, 1966.

Mayer, Harold M., and Wade, Richard C. *Chicago: Growth of a Metropolis*. Chicago: University of Chicago Press, 1969.

Mayers, Lewis. *The American Legal System*. New York: Harper, 1955.

McGlothian, William J. *Patterns of Professional Education*. New York: G. P. Putnam's Sons, 1960.

————. *The Professional Schools*. New York: Center for Applied Research in Education, Inc., 1964.

Miller, Perry, ed. *The Legal Mind in America: From Independence to the Civil War*. Garden City, New York: Doubleday, 1962.

Moore, Philip S. *A Century of Law at Notre Dame*. Notre Dame: University of Notre Dame Press, 1970.

My Philosophy of Law: Credos of Sixteen American Scholars. Boston: Boston Law Book Company, 1941.

Morison, Samuel Eliot. *The Oxford History of the American People*. New York: Oxford University Press, 1965.

Nevins, Allan. *John D. Rockefeller, the Heroic Age of American Enterprise*. 2 vols. New York: Charles Scribner's Sons, 1940.

————. *The State Universities and Democracy*. Urbana: University of Illinois Press, 1962.

————. *Study in Power, John D. Rockefeller, Industrialist and Philanthropist*. 2 vols. New York: Charles Scribner's Sons, 1953.

Packer, Herbert L., and Ehrlich, Thomas. *New Directions in Legal Education*. Carnegie Commission on Higher Education Reports. New York: McGraw-Hill, 1972.

Patridge, Bellamy. *County Lawyer*. New York: Whittlesey House, 1939.

Philadelphia Bar Association. Recording the Proceedings, Addresses, and Historical Displays and Observances Incident to the Commemoration of the 150th Anniversary of the Association, 1802–1952. Philadelphia: Philadelphia Bar Association, 1952.

———. *Addresses Delivered March 13, 1902, and Papers Prepared or Republished To Commemorate the Centennial Celebration of the Law Association of Philadelphia, Pennsylvania, 1802–1902.* Philadelphia: Law Association of Philadelphia, 1906.

Phillips, Orie L., and McCoy, Philbrick. *Conduct of Judges and Lawyers: A Study of Professional Ethics, Discipline and Disbarment.* Los Angeles, Published for the Survey of the Legal Profession by Parker, 1952.

Pierce, Bessie Louise. *A History of Chicago.* 3 vols. New York: A. A. Knopf, 1937–57.

Pierson, George Wilson. *Yale College: An Educational History.* New Haven: Yale University Press, 1952.

Portraits of the American University, 1890–1910. Compiled by James C. Stone and Donald P. DeNevi. San Francisco: Jossey-Bass, 1971.

Pound, Roscoe. *The History and System of the Common Law.* New York: P. F. Collier, 1939.

———. *The Lawyer from Antiquity to Modern Times.* St. Paul: West Publishing Company, 1953.

Proceedings of the Annual Meeting of the American Bar Association. Philadelphia: Dando Press, 1890–1902.

Professional Education in the United States: Statistics of Professional and Allied Schools. Washington, D.C.: Government Printing Office, 1896.

Rahl, James A., and Schwerin, Kurt. *Northwestern University School of Law: A Short History.* Chicago: privately printed, 1960.

Rainsford, George N. *Congress and Higher Education in the Nineteenth Century.* Knoxville: University of Tennessee Press, 1972.

Redlich, Josef. *The Common Law and the Case Method in*

American University Law Schools. Bull. no. 8. New York: Carnegie Foundation for the Advancement of Teaching, 1915.

Reed, Alfred Z. *Present Day Law Schools in the United States and Canada*. Bull. no. 21. New York: Carnegie Foundation for the Advancement of Teaching, 1928.

——. *Training for the Public Profession of the Law*. Bull. no. 15. New York: Carnegie Foundation for the Advancement of Teaching, 1921.

Reisner, Edward H. *Nationalism and Education Since 1789*. New York: Macmillan, 1922.

Report of the Committee on Legal Education, American Bar Association. Philadelphia: Dando Press, 1890–99.

Rippa, S. Alexander. *Education in a Free Society*. New York: David McKay, 1971.

Roosevelt, Theodore. *The Letters of Theodore Roosevelt*, ed. Elting R. Morison. 8 vols. Cambridge: Harvard University Press, 1951–54.

Rudolph, Frederick. *The American College and University: A History*. New York: Alfred A. Knopf, 1962.

Schweinburg, Eric F. *Law Training in Continental Europe*. New York: Russell Sage Foundation, 1945.

Selected Readings on the Legal Profession. St. Paul: West Publishing Company, 1962.

Stone, Julius. *Legal Education and Public Responsibility*. Washington, D.C.: Association of American Law Schools, 1959.

Storr, Richard J. *The Beginnings of Graduate Education in the United States*. Chicago: University of Chicago Press, 1953.

Sunderland, Edson R. *History of The American Bar Association and Its Work*. Privately printed, 1953.

Sutherland, Arthur E. *The Law at Harvard, a History of Ideas and Men, 1817–1967*. Cambridge: Harvard University Press, Belknap Press, 1967.

Swaine, Robert I. *The Cravath Firm and Its Predecessors, 1819–1947*. 2 vols. New York: Ad Press, 1946–48.

Taft, Henry W. *A Century and a Half at the New York Bar:*

Being the Annals of a Law Firm and Sketches of Its Members. New York: privately printed, 1938.

Taylor, Henry L. *Professional Education in the United States*. Albany: University of the State of New York, 1900.

Thwing, Charles F. *A History of Higher Education*. New York: Appleton, 1906.

Tinnelly, Joseph T. *Part-Time Legal Education: A Study of the Problems of Evening Law Schools*. Brooklyn, New York: Foundation Press, 1957.

Tocqueville, Alexis de. *Democracy in America*, ed. Phillips Bradley. 2 vols. New York: Alfred A. Knopf, 1945.

Twining, William. *Karl Llewellyn and the Realist Movement*. London: Weidenfeld and Nicolson, 1973.

Veblen, Thorstein. *The Higher Learning in America*. New York: B. W. Huebsch, 1918.

———. *The Theory of the Leisure Class*. New York: Macmillan, 1899.

Veysey, Laurence R. *The Emergence of the American University*. Chicago: University of Chicago Press, 1965.

Warren, Charles. *History of the Harvard Law School and of Early Legal Conditions in America*. New York, 1908. Reprint. 2 vols. New York: De Capo Press, 1970.

———. *A History of the American Bar*. Boston, 1911. Reprint. New York: Howard Fertig, 1966.

Who's Who in Jurisprudence. New York: John W. Leonard Corporation, 1925.

Women in the Law. An Analysis of Training, Practice, and Salaried Positions. New York: The Bureau of Vocational Information, 1920.

C. Articles

Abbott, Austin. "Existing Questions on Legal Education." *Yale Law Journal* 3 (1893): 1–16.

Ames, James Barr. "The Vocation of the Law Professor." *American Law Register* 48 (1906): 129.

Anderson, Robert B. "Memoir, Inside the Law School, 1892–1938." *Harvard Law School Bulletin* 16 (1965): 8.

Arnold, Isaac N. "Recollections of Early Chicago and the Illinois Bar." *Chicago Bar Association Lectures.* Chicago: Fergus Printing Company, 1882.

"Attorneys and Their Education." *Irish Quarterly Review* (1857): p. 29.

Auerbach, Jerold S. "Enmity and Amity: Law Teachers and Practitioners, 1900–1922." In *Perspectives in American History* (1972), pp. 551–601.

Babb, James E. "Union College of Law." *The Green Bag* 1 (1899): 330–38.

Baldwin, Simeon E. "Graduate Courses, at Law Schools." *Journal of Social Science* 11 (1880): 123–37.

———. "Law School Libraries, and How to Use Them." *Report of the Committee on Legal Education, American Bar Association* (1894): 431–38.

———. "The Re-Adjustment of the Collegiate to the Professional Course." *Yale Law Journal* 8 (1898): 1–15.

———. "The Study of Elementary Law, The Proper Beginning of a Legal Education." *Yale Law Journal* 8 (1903): 1–15.

Ball, Harry V. "Re-examination of William Graham Sumner on Law and Social Change." *Journal of Legal Education* 14 (1962): 299–316.

Ballantine, Henry W. "The Place in Legal Education of Evening and Correspondence Schools." *American Law School Review* 4 (1919): 369.

Beale, Joseph H., Jr. "The Development of Jurisprudence During the Past Century." *Harvard Law Review* 18 (1905): 271–83.

———. "The Place of Professional Education in the Universities." *University Record* 9 (1905): 42–47.

Bigelow, Melville M. "A Scientific School of Legal Thought." *The Green Bag* 17 (1905): 1–11.

Bloomfield, Maxwell. "Law vs. Politics: The Self-Image of the

American Bar, 1830–1860." *American Journal of Legal History* 13 (1968): 306–23.

———. "Lawyers and Public Criticism: Challenge and Response in Nineteenth-Century America." *American Journal of Legal History* 15 (1971): 269–77.

Bremer, David J. "A Better Education, The Great Need of the Profession." *Yale Law Journal* 5 (1895): 1–13.

Bristol, George W. "The Passing of the Legal Profession." *Yale Law Journal* 22 (1912–13): 590–613.

Bruce, Andrew Alexander. "The Function of the State University Law School." *Michigan Law Review* 5 (1906): 1–5.

Burdick, Francis M. "Half Century of Legal Education." *Cornell Law Quarterly* 4 (1919): 138–42.

Butler, Nicholas Murray. "The Length of the College Course." In *Present College Questions*. New York: D. Appleton & Company, 1903, pp. 95–105.

Campbell, Enid. "German Influences in English Legal Education and Jurisprudence in the 19th Century." *American Law Review* 4 (1959): 357–77.

Cardozo, Michael H. "Accreditation of Law Schools in the United States." *Journal of Legal Education* 18 (1966): 420–24.

Carter, James C. "Address." *Harvard Law School Association: Report of the Ninth Annual Meeting, June 25, 1895, in especial honor of Christopher Columbus Langdell*. Boston: Harvard Law School Association, 1895, pp. 5–10.

Casper, Gerhard. "Two Models of Legal Education." *Tennessee Law Review* 51 (1973): 13–25.

Chapin. "The Decline of the Practicing Lawyer." *National Corporation Reporter* 25 (1902): 69.

Choate, Rufus. "The Position and Functions of the American Bar, As An Element of Conservation in the State." In Perry Miller, ed. *The Legal Mind in America: From Independence to the Civil War*. Garden City, New York: Doubleday, 1962, pp. 258–73.

Chroust, Anton-Hermann. "The Emergence of Professional

Standards and the Rise of the Legal Profession—The Graeco-Roman Period." *Boston University Law Review* 36 (1956): 587–91.

Clark, E. C. "Jurisprudence: Its Use and Its Place in Legal Education." *Law Quarterly Review* 1 (1885): 201–6.

Clark, Herbert W. "A Proud Record in Legal Education; The Milestones in its Evolution." *American Bar Journal* 39 (1953): 730–35.

Conkling, James C. "Recollections of the Bench and the Bar of Central Illinois." *Chicago Bar Association Lectures*. Chicago: Fergus Printing Company, 1882.

Cooley, Roger W. "Manual Training for Lawyers." *American Law School Review* 2 (1909): 261–65.

Corbin, Arthur L. "Yale and the New School of Jurisprudence." *Case and Comment* 21 (1915): 953–62.

Cornish, Louis C. "The Student Rows of Oxford, With Some Hints of Their Significance." *The Green Bag* 16 (1904): 651.

Currie, Brainerd. "The Materials of Law Study." *Journal of Legal Education* 3 (1951): 331–83.

————. "The Place of Law in the Liberal Arts College." In *Conference on The Profession of Law and Legal Education*. University of Chicago Law School Conference Series, vol. 16. Chicago: University of Chicago Law School, 1952.

Deak, Francis. "French Legal Education and Some Reflections on Legal Education in the United States." *Wisconsin Law Review* 14 (1939): 473–95.

Dewey, John. "Pedagogy as a University Discipline." *University Record* 1 (1896): 354.

Dexter, Edwin G. "The Educational Status of the Legal Profession." *The Green Bag* 15 (1903): 217–22.

Dicey, A. V. "Teaching of English Law at Harvard." *Harvard Law Review* 13 (1900): 422–40.

Dill, James B. "The Law Has Changed Radically." *Law Student's Helper* 8 (1900): 790.

Dillon, John F. "The True Professional Ideal." *Report of the*

Committee on Legal Education, American Bar Association (1894), pp. 417–22.

Dodge, Emily P. "Evolution of a City Law Office." *Wisconsin Law Review* 31 (1955): 180–207; 32 (1956): 35–56.

Dowd, Willis B. "Some Delights of the Legal Profession." *The Green Bag* 8 (1901): 417–25.

Eliot, Charles W. "Address." In *Harvard Law School Association, Report of the Ninth Annual Meeting, June 25, 1895, in especial honor of Christopher Columbus Langdell.* Boston: Harvard Law School Association, 1895, pp. 11–16.

———. "The Length of the College Course." In *Present College Questions.* New York: D. Appleton, 1903, pp. 47–59.

"Ernst Freund—Pioneer of Administrative Law." *University of Chicago Law Review* 29 (1962): 755–81.

Field, David Dudley. "Reform in the Legal Profession and the Laws." In Perry Miller, ed. *The Legal Mind in America: From Independence to the Civil War.* Garden City, New York: Doubleday, 1962, pp. 285–95.

Finch, F. M. "Legal Education." *Columbia Law Review* 1 (1901): 94–107.

Frankfurter, Felix. "Joseph Henry Beale." *Harvard Law Review* 56 (1943): 701–3.

Freund, Ernst. "The Correlation of Work for Higher Degrees in Graduate School and Law School." *Illinois Law Review* 11 (1916): 301–10.

———. "Study of Law in Germany." *Counsellor* 1 (1891): 131.

Frost, E. Allen. "Advice to Students at Law in the Year 1668." *The Green Bag* 4 (1892): 446–67.

G., E. M. W. A. "The Teaching of Law in Correspondence Schools." *The Green Bag* 22 (1910): 198.

Garrison, Lloyd K. "A Survey of the Wisconsin Bar." *Wisconsin Law Review* 10 (1935): 131–69.

Geis, Gilbert. "Thorstein Veblen on Legal Education." *Journal of Legal Education* 10 (1957): 62–67.

Gilmore, E. A. "The Preliminary Education of the Law Student." *American Lawyer* 15 (1907): 428–30.

Glanville, W. E. "The Study of Law from the Standpoints of Mental Discipline and Good Citizenship." *The Green Bag* 9 (1897): 301–4.

Gregory, Charles Noble. "The Wage of Law Teachers." *Law Quarterly Review* 14 (1898): 34.

Griffith, Ogden E. "The Value of Correspondence Instruction in Law." *American Law School Review* 2 (1907): 166–74.

Griswold, Erwin N. "Mr. Beale and the Conflict of Laws." *Harvard Law Review* 56 (1943): 690–94.

———. "English and American Legal Education." *Journal of Legal Education* 10 (1958): 429–36.

———. "The Future of Legal Education." In *Conference on The Profession of Law and Legal Education.* University of Chicago Law School Conference Series, vol. 16. Chicago: University of Chicago Law School, 1952, pp. 99–110.

Hall, James Parker. "American Law School Degrees." *Michigan Law Review* 6 (1907): 112–17.

———. "Practice Work in Law Schools." *The Green Bag* 17 (1905): 528–34.

Hall, Oakey. "English and American Bar in Contrast." *The Green Bag* 5 (1893): 237.

Hand, August W. "Julian W. Mack." *Harvard Law Review* 57 (1943): 96–97.

Harno, Albert J. "Ideas and the Law." *American Bar Association Journal* 26 (1940): 651–52.

Harper, William Rainey. "Coeducation" (1905); "The Contribution of Johns Hopkins" (1903); "Dependence of the West Upon the East" (1901); "The Length of the College Course" (1905); "The Old and New in Education" (1894); "The Situation of the Small College" (1900); "Some Present Tendencies of Popular Education" (1905); "The University and Democracy" (1899); "The Urban University" (1902); "Waste in Higher Education" (1899). Speeches made by Harper between 1894 and 1905 and published by the

University of Chicago Press, 1902, in *The Trend in Higher Education*.

———. "The Trend of University and College Education in the United States." *North American Review* 175 (1902): 457–65.

Hepburn, Charles M. "The Modern Law School in England and America." *Virginia Law Review* 2 (1914): 85–97.

Hezeltine, Harold D. "Law Schools and Legal Practitioners in America." *Law Quarterly Review* 33 (1917): 309–34.

Holmes, Oliver Wendell. "Dedication—1897; the Path of the Law." *Boston University Law Review* 33 (1917): 309–34.

Hoyne, Thomas. "The Lawyer as a Pioneer." *Chicago Bar Association Lectures*. Chicago: Fergus Printing Company, 1882.

———. "Reminiscences of Thomas M. Hoyne." *The [Northwestern] Alumni Journal* 16 (1916): 28–31.

Hurst, Willard. "A Historian Views the Profession." In *Conference on The Profession of Law and Legal Education*. University of Chicago Law School Conference Series, vol. 16. Chicago: University of Chicago Law School, 1952, pp. 75–84.

Hutchins, Harry B. "Humanistic and Particularly Classical Studies as Preparation for the Law." *Michigan Law Review* 5 (1907): 545–50.

Irvine, R. T. "The Lawyer of the Future." In *Proceedings of the Virginia Bar Association* (1900), pp. 275–98.

"Is Apprenticeship in a Law Office Desirable while Pursuing a Course of Study in a Law School." *American Law School Review* 1 (1903): 89–91.

Jackson, James. "Law and Lawyers. Is the Profession of the Advocate Consistent with Perfect Integrity." *Knickerbocker Magazine* 28 (1846): 378–83.

Jethro, Brown W. "The American Law School." *Law Quarterly Review* 21 (1905): 69–78.

Johnson, William R. "Education and Professional Life Styles: Law and Medicine in the Nineteenth Century." *History of Education Quarterly* 14 (1974): 185–208.

Jones, William. "The American Legal Method: Its Relevance to the Process of National Method." *Journal of Legal Education* 21 (1968): 71–75.

Kaestle, Carl F. "Social Reform and the Urban School." *History of Education Quarterly* 12 (1972): 211–28.

Kales, Albert M. "The Economic Basis for a Society of Advocates in the City of Chicago." *Illinois Law Review* 9 (1915): 478–88.

Kent, Arthur H. "Ernst Freund—Jurist and Social Scientist." *Journal of Political Economy* 41 (1933): 145–51.

Lawson, John D. "Some Standards of Legal Education in the West." In *Report of the 1894 Annual Meeting of the American Bar Association* (1894), pp. 423–30.

Ledlie, J. C. "Legal Education: A Suggestion from Germany." *Law Quarterly Review* 30 (1914): 46.

Lee, Blewett. "Teaching Practice in Law Schools." *Report of the 1896 Annual Meeting of the American Bar Association* (1896), pp. 507–20.

Lee, Edward T. "The Evening Law School." *American Law School Review* 1 (1905): 290–95.

"Legal Education." *The Green Bag* 3 (1891): 516–24.

Levi, Edward H. "The Political, the Professional and the Prudent." *Journal of Legal Education* 11 (1959): 457–69.

Lewinski, Karl von. "The Education of the German Lawyer." *The Green Bag* 20 (1908): 11–14.

Lorenzen, E. G. "Seminary Methods of Legal Instruction at the University of Berlin." *American Law School Review* 1 (1906): 388–95.

Lundberg, Ferdinand. "Law Factories." *Harper's Magazine* (July, 1939), p. 180.

MacLean, George E. "The Relation of Professional Schools to College Work." *University Record* 6 (1901–2): 30–33.

Mansfield, E. G. "Ambulance Chasing—The Other Side." *Law Student's Helper* 13 (1905): 306–10.

Mayer, Levy. "Has Commercialism Impaired the Lawyer of

Today." *Proceedings of the Illinois State Bar Association* (1900), pp. 101–7.

McCaul, Robert L. "Dewey and the University of Chicago." *School and Society* 79 (1961): 152–57; 179–83; 202–6.

McIlwraith, Malcolm. "French Schools of Law." *Law Quarterly Review* 6 (1890): 42–44.

Mechem, Floyd R. "The Opportunities and Responsibilities of the American Law School." *Michigan Law Review* 5 (1907): 344–53.

Murphy, William A. "The Lawyer's Fees." *Law Student's Helper* 12 (1914): 4–7.

Nash, Gary B. "The Philadelphia Bench and Bar, 1800–1861." *Comparative Studies in Society and History* 7 (1965): 203–20.

Neal, Phil C. "De Tocqueville and the Role of the Lawyer in Society." *Marquette Law Review* 50 (1967): 607–17.

"Parisian Law-Student Life." *The Green Bag* 1 (1889): 511–12.

Pattee, William S. "Law School of the University of Minnesota." *The Green Bag* 2 (1890): 203–14.

Patten, Simon N. "The New Jurisprudence." *University of Pennsylvania Law Review* 62 (1913): 17–33.

Platt, Robert R. "The Decadence of Law as a Profession and Its Growth as a Business." *Yale Law Journal* 12 (1903): 441–45.

Pound, Roscoe. "Achievement of the American Law School." *Dicta* 38 (1961): 269–73.

———. "Joseph Henry Beale." *Harvard Law Review* 56 (1943): 695–98.

———. "The Law and the People." *University of Chicago Magazine* 3 (1910): 1–16.

———. "The Law School and the Professional Tradition." *Michigan Law Review* 24 (1925): 156–65.

Prashker, Louis. "Legal Education in the United States—A Critique of Dean Harno's Report Prepared For the Survey of the Legal Profession." *St. John's Law Review* 28 (1953): 30–45.

"Presidential Lawyers." *The Green Bag* 9 (1897): 104–5.

Raynolds, Edward V. "Legal Education in Germany." *Yale Law Journal* 12 (1902): 31–34.

Reinhard, George L. "American Law Schools and the Teaching of Law." *The Green Bag* 16 (1904): 165–70.

"Report on the Committee on Disbarment." In *Proceedings of the Iowa State Bar Association* (1914), pp. 168–69.

Rheinstein, Max. "The Case Method of Legal Education: The First One-Hundred Years." [University of Chicago] *Law School Record* 21 (1975): 3–15.

———. "Integration of Matter Not Strictly Legal in European Legal Education." *American Law School Review* 8 (1937): 718–34.

———. "Law Faculties and Law Schools: A Comparison of Legal Education in the United States and Germany." *Wisconsin Law Review* 13 (1938): 5–42.

Richberg, Donald R. "The Lawyer's Function." *Atlantic Monthly* 104 (1909): 489–92.

Riesenfeld, Stefan. "A Comparison of Continental and American Legal Education." *Michigan Law Review* 36 (1937): 31–55.

Robison, Lelia J. "Women Lawyers in the United States." *The Green Bag* 2 (1890): 1–32.

Rogers, Henry Wade. "Address." In *Report of the 1890 Annual Meeting of the American Bar Association* (1890), pp. 1–14.

Russell, Lord, of Killowen. "The Bar as a Profession." *Irish Monthly* 30 (1902): 459.

Schirrmeister, Gustav. "Legal Education in Germany." *Law Magazine and Review* 13 (1945): 71–89.

Seagle, William. "Rudolph von Jhering: Or Law as a Means to an End." *University of Chicago Law Review* 13 (1945): 71–89.

Shelton, George F. "Law as a Business." *Yale Law Journal* 10 (1900): 275–83.

Smith, Frank C. "Incompetency of Lawyers." In *Professional*

Education in the United States, Henry L. Taylor. Albany: University of the State of New York, 1900, pp. 1252–53.

Smith, George Harris. "History of the Activity of the American Bar Association in Relation to Legal Education and Admission to the Bar." *American Law School Review* 7 (1930): 1–34.

Steffens, Lincoln. "The Shame of Minneapolis: The Rescue and Redemption of a City That Was Sold Out." *McClure's Magazine* 20 (1903): 228–39.

Stevens, Robert. "Two Cheers for 1870: The American Law School." *Perspectives in American History* (1972): 405–548.

Thayer, James Bradley. "The Teaching of English Law at Universities." *Harvard Law Review* 9 (1895): 169–73.

Treat, Samuel. "A Nineteenth Century View of the Study of Law." *St. Louis Law Review* 9 (1923): 23–30.

Tucker, John Randolph. "What Is the Best Training for the American Bar of the Future." *Proceedings of the 1896 Annual Meeting of the American Bar Association* (1896), pp. 595–605.

Turner [Steffen], Roscoe. "Changing Objectives in Legal Education." *Yale Law Journal* 40 (1930): 576–84.

Walker, John Brisben. "Making A Choice of a Profession, The Law." *Cosmopolitan* 34 (1903): 351–54.

Wetmore, Edmund. "Some of the Limitations and Requirements of Legal Education in the United States." *Proceedings of the 1894 Annual Meeting of the American Bar Association* (1894), pp. 461–68.

Whitaker, Frederic Earle. "The Study of Old Greek Law." *The Green Bag* 17 (1905): 95–99.

White, Edward B. "Changed Conditions in the Practice of Law." *Reports of the New York State Bar Association* (1904): pp. 114–22.

White, James J. "Women in the Law." *Michigan Law Review* 65 (1967): 1051–1122.

Wilgus, H. L. "Legal Education in the United States." *Michigan Law Review* 6 (1908): 647–82.

Williams, F. B. "Civil Law in Law Schools." *Western Reserve Law Journal* 5 (1899): 150–56.

Williston, Samuel. "Joseph Henry Beale: A Biographical Sketch." *Harvard Law Review* 56 (1943): 686–89.

Wilson, Woodrow. "Legal Education of Undergraduates." *Proceedings of the 1894 Annual Meeting of the American Bar Association* (1894), pp. 439–51.

Woodward, Frederic. "Ernst Freund." *University Record* 19 (1933): 39–42.

Index